The Practitioner's Guide to

USER EXPERIENCE DESIGN

Also from General Assembly

The Practitioner's Guide to Product Management

The Practitioner's Guide to Web Development

The Practitioner's Guide to

USER EXPERIENCE DESIGN

Luke Miller

PIATKUS

First published in the US in 2015 by Grand
Central Publishing, a division of Hachette Book Group, Inc.
First published in Great Britain in 2015 by Piatkus

1 3 5 7 9 10 8 6 4 2

A CIP catalogue record for this book
is available from the British Library.

ISBN 978-0-349-40677-0

Printed and bound by CPI Group (UK) Ltd, Croydon, CR0 4YY

Papers used by Piatkus are from well-managed forests
and other responsible sources.

Piatkus
An imprint of
Little, Brown Book Group
100 Victoria Embankment
London EC4Y 0DY

An Hachette UK Company
www.hachette.co.uk

www.piatkus.co.uk

CONTENTS

FOREWORD

When my cofounders and I started General Assembly in 2010, our vision for the company went well beyond offering classes in web technology; we wanted to empower a global community of individuals to pursue work they love. Our concept was to offer an easily accessible point of entry for people who wanted to get into the dynamic tech scene, or to add to their skills, or perhaps to make a career change or move into a new area in tech. We focused on creating classes taught in a hands-on, learning-by-doing style by people who were themselves immersed in the scene and could offer a wealth of experienced-based insights.

Since then, our small startup space has grown into a global education provider, with nine campuses on four continents, offering a wide range of courses in web development, UX design, product management, entrepreneurship, data science, and more, including everything from full-time immersive courses to short workshops. We continue to evolve our offerings, and with this series of books we've asked some of our most popular instructors to distill their wisdom into lively introductions that provide a real-world understanding of the exciting fields they work in.

UX Design was one of the first courses we launched, and it quickly became a hit. We had seen in the burgeoning New York City tech community that design had become a key differentiator for startups hoping to disrupt legacy industries. Many of the most successful companies, from Reddit to Etsy and Tumblr, did not start with the idea of improving a supply chain or disintermediating a complex transaction.

Rather, they looked at how to improve the customer's experience in ways that would surprise and delight: the essential mission of UX.

We also found that there was a clear gap in the market—actually in *two* markets: startups and other employers had no clear way to find skilled UX designers, and aspiring UX designers had no easy way to acquire skills. It was the old catch-22 of "you can't get a job without experience, and you can't get experience without a job." This is one of the essential problems General Assembly tries to solve for many parts of the twenty-first-century economy.

This book helps to fill the gap by introducing what UX is all about and how anyone can begin the journey to expertise in the field, or how those who already have some experience in UX design can supplement their skills to take their work to a new level. The book reveals one of the most creative and in-demand areas of tech today, a vital ingredient in the success of the most innovative businesses around the world. We hope you'll use it to create great experiences for your users and everyone else around you.

—Jake Schwartz
CEO, General Assembly

INTRODUCTION

This is a great time to learn about user experience (UX) design. The core mission of UX is to craft digital experiences that not only empower but delight users, and we've never had a better set of tools for doing so. There is strong demand in digital product development for people with the skills, and technology is evolving so rapidly and in such interesting ways that the work affords constant opportunities to innovate and let your creativity run. The move to mobile began only a few years ago, and a whole new era of even more innovative digital products is already dawning.

Think of the possibilities for the experiences that can be created for the living room of the future, as envisioned by Sony. That company recently unveiled its Life Space UX project, which will turn all the surfaces of our homes into rich visual displays. In the midst of a cold, rainy day, the technology will allow us to project an image of a skylight on our ceilings, bathing our rooms in the warming glow of a bright spring morning. Rather than books on bookshelves we'll have interactive images projected on our walls of our vast arrays of ebooks, music, games, and videos, and our kitchen counters and coffee tables will be tablet computers. Assuming it takes off, the Google Glass device will be offering its own wealth of opportunities for innovating. We'll have to create experiences that users interact with in ways that don't currently exist. And personal assistant robots may soon be populating our homes, and will need to be made comfortable to be around rather than slightly creepy.

Maybe you can be the one to figure out a great new look and feel for products on web TV. Or you could be in the vanguard of developing the just emerging "Internet of Things," making all the mundane objects of our daily lives highly responsive to our needs and desires. Maybe you'll get to work on the next generation of windows, which will be sensitive to light and air quality and will open or close or draw their shades automatically.

But how do you get into UX design? Do you have to know how to write code? Or do you need a degree in design? And what exactly is UX? I'm asked these questions all the time. The truth is that even people in UX have differing views of the best way to describe UX. Is UX a noun or a verb? Does it refer to the process or the result? And UX is practiced in all sorts of different ways at different places. The confusion isn't helped by the proliferation of arcane terms that have been used to refer to those who do UX research and design: *interaction designer*, *information architect*, *usability engineer*, *usability analyst*, *UX strategist*, and *user research specialist* are only a few of the ways you might see jobs in the field described. What's more, the same terms are used for jobs that have widely varying sets of responsibilities. What an information architect will be asked to do at one company may be quite different from what other firms request.

The term *user experience designer* is becoming the preferred language, but at the same time, UX expertise is increasingly being added to the job descriptions for other specialties in digital product development. In particular, the hybrid job of UX developer is rapidly emerging, blending expertise in front-end coding with UX research and design skills. And at many startups, there is no budget for a UX specialist, and the designers are expected to be jacks-of-all-trades and to seamlessly work UX into the development process. So whether you want to work in UX full-time, as I've done with the *Wall Street Journal* and at Yahoo, or just want to add UX to your areas of expertise, this is a great time to learn about UX. Not only will doing so make you more marketable, but a knowledge of UX principles and practices can enrich your work in any part of digital product creation.

No matter whether you're just starting out in digital work or are already established as a visual designer, a back-end or front-end developer, or a product manager, if you are in web and app development I strongly encourage you to learn the craft. If you're a visual designer, incorporating UX methods into your work will enhance your ability to please users with your designs by tapping into their emotions and putting yourself in their place. It will also help you in presenting your design concepts and gaining support for them, as well as in working with the development team to bring them to fruition. If you're a front-end developer, UX practices will help you create more effective and pleasing interfaces with the evidence in hand that they're meeting the users' needs and desires. Even for developers working on the back-end systems, an understanding of the insights of UX will help in anticipating ways to optimize the structure of databases and the capabilities of systems to enable innovations that enhance the user experience.

So what is UX and how do you do it? The best answer to the first question is that UX is both a noun and a verb; it's both the end result experience a product offers and a set of methods with which to craft experiences. Those methods include user research techniques, such as conducting user interviews and surveys, creating personas to represent the range of users you're appealing to, and performing competitive analysis of rival products. They also include a core set of specifications for crafting well-designed routes of navigation through sites and apps, called user flows. Additional techniques include designing the layouts and interface elements of pages, from initial sketching, to creating a rough site architecture, on to drawing the more detailed page designs generally called wireframes and then making moving prototypes. Finally, UX work involves user testing, which can be done with anything from rough sketches to fully functioning prototypes. The UX designer must interpret the results of tests and make recommendations for any changes to products that are indicated.

In this book, I'll introduce you to each of these methods, drawing on my own experiences and telling stories of specific projects that illuminate what the day-to-day work of a UX designer is like. I'll focus on the lessons I've learned, oftentimes the hard way, and I'll offer hands-on tips about the ins and outs of practicing the methods. Because, as they say, the devil is in the details, I'll discuss a host of specific examples of designs of actual products, decoding the good, the bad, and the ugly of UX.

Though I'll give you a good grounding in the basic UX design principles and how to practice the methods—and this book will allow you to dive right into doing so—I think it's important not to think of UX as the sum of its methodological parts. UX is also a way of thinking and seeing, and it involves grappling with a number of larger and quite tricky business issues that I'll address. One of the most challenging of those, and one of the most important mandates of good UX, is knowing when it's appropriate to innovate. When should you introduce a new interaction or craft a custom design element, and when is it better to rely on the tried and true? I'll examine how to draw that line.

Another tricky question is when, if ever, business requirements should outweigh user goals. And one of the most pressing issues UX designers face is how to help the members of development teams better understand what UX design has to offer so they're more receptive to ideas. I'll delve into each of these topics and offer tips I've found very helpful in grappling with these issues. And finally, I'll discuss how seeing through the lens of UX allows you to spot good ideas for product design everywhere, whether in the beautiful symmetry of the rings of Saturn, the playful whimsy of a children's amusement park, or the collaborative process of making a movie with friends.

The best UX comes from learning by doing, and one of the things I wish were better understood about the work is how creative, fun, and satisfying it can be. UX design is a dynamic, fast-evolving field, and the doors are open. The best answer to the question of how to get into UX design is simply this: begin. I hope this book will inspire you to do so.

Chapter 1

SEEING THROUGH USERS' EYES

I made my way into user experience design through an unexpected route. My interest dates back to an undergraduate English class I took on the master of suspense, Alfred Hitchcock. I thought it would be fun and easy; after all, the required reading included textbooks with titles like *Men, Women, and Chainsaws*. As a prepharmacy major at the time, I needed at least one class that would be a breeze. Little did I know how fascinating I would find learning the details of how storytellers created such thrilling experiences for viewers.

I ended up loving Hitchcock. We studied how he composed his shots and the narrative tricks he used to steer viewers' eyes to exactly what he wanted them to pay attention to and increase the mystery and tension of scenes. In *Rear Window*, he limits the audience's view to that from the apartment of Jimmy Stewart's character, L. B. Jefferies. We watch through the binoculars of the wheelchair-bound Mr. Jefferies as a murder mystery unfolds in the apartment across the courtyard, catching only suggestive glimpses of the grisly deeds his neighbor may be perpetrating. What's the man done with that large knife and the handsaw he's cleaning? Is Jefferies merely falling prey to an overwrought imagination? The voyeuristic viewpoint puts us right in the mystery. And, of course, who could ever forget the tension of the scene in *Psycho* where Hitchcock places us in the shower with Janet Leigh? As we look out through the shower curtain, we see only a shadowy silhouette of the bathroom door opening and the murderer approaching. It's one of the scariest shots in all of film. The full scene was so complex that it required seventy-eight different shot setups, and the effect was so compelling that it's said to have caused a new phobia of taking showers. For me, the experience of the class was so transformative that I changed my major to English.

Hitchcock's achievement became all the more impressive to me when I learned in later classes about how different people's readings are of any given "text," whether a novel, a movie scene, or, as I was to find years later when I got into UX design, a website or app. We studied different methods of reading a text, which the literary theorist Stanley Fish called interpretive strategies. I loved discovering how various schools of thought read a novel or play, learning to appreciate the multitude of ways people perceive.

Fish emphasized that an individual's approach to any text is very much a matter of her life experiences and perspectives. He stressed that it's important not to insist on the correctness of one person's interpretation over another's. That contention earned him notoriety and a good deal of derision by those who thought his argument was extreme. The literary critic David Hirsch described Fish as "hopelessly alienated from art, from truth, and from humanity."[1] But I appreciated how he helped me see through others' eyes and to enjoy that feeling of ambivalence I get when my own interpretation is met with a well-marshaled set of opposing facts. I learned to empathize and see someone else's perspective, which has been invaluable in my becoming a good UX practitioner. Different people experience apps and sites differently, and the more we are able to appreciate those differences and adapt our designs to them, the better user experiences we'll create.

YOU'RE NOT DESIGNING FOR YOU

The most valuable lesson I've learned as a UX designer has been that the ways users interact with a product and the experiences they have with it vary wildly depending on their backgrounds and life situations. Is the user a baby boomer, or a ten-year-old just learning to search the web? Is she coming to your site or app while she's at home watching TV or on the train commuting to work? Is she a new mother who has very little time to shop and just wants to order her diapers from your site as quickly as possible, or is she a fashionista who loves spending lots of time looking through the latest designer offerings?

A memorable story I heard once speaks volumes about just how much the context of our experience can shape our perceptions. It concerns a huge power outage that hit Los Angeles. The city went entirely dark, and a flood of alarmed calls came in to the astronomical observatory in Griffith Park asking what was falling out of the sky. It turned out that because of all of the ambient light that's normally in the sky over L.A. during the night, the callers had never seen the sky really full of stars before. They were terrified.

You never want to underestimate how unfamiliar some features you want to build may be to users. My generation (Y) and those that follow me are already familiar with touch screens because we started interacting with them as soon as they came online. But for others, the technology is still very new, and they don't know all the things touch screens allow them to do or the wealth of features that have been created for them. Even swiping may feel odd and unintuitive to them. With the learning curve as high as it is for these users, it's our job as UX designers to remove any extra thinking from their interaction with our products that is not central to what they want or need to do.

Of course, touch screen interactions will become familiar to everyone before long. And that's another key thing UX designers must always keep in mind: there is always going to be a new learning curve to be aware of, as long as the world sees innovations in computing.

The history of people failing to grasp how to make use of new features in technology is replete with almost mind-boggling stories. Here's an example that's become somewhat famous in tech circles from a hilarious article by *Wall Street Journal* reporter Jim Carlton, recounting a number of tech support calls:

> The exasperated help-line caller said she couldn't get her new Dell computer to turn on. Jay Alblinger, a Dell Computer Corp. technician, made sure the computer was plugged in and then asked the woman what happened when she pushed the power button.
>
> "I've pushed and pushed on this foot pedal and nothing happens," the woman replied. "Foot pedal?" the technician asked. "Yes," the woman said, "this little white foot pedal with the on switch."
>
> The "foot pedal," it turned out, was the computer's mouse.[2]

Here's another howler, which was posted on the site Rinkworks.com:

> I had a job at my local school board doing on-site technical support. We had just recently replaced all the Macintosh machines with Windows NT machines. While showing one of the secretaries the Windows environment, she asked where all of her icons were. I pointed to the two columns of icons on the left side of her screen.
>
> HER: Yes, but on my Mac they were all over here on the right.
> ME: Well, by default, Windows arranges the columns on the left side.
> HER: But I'm right-handed![3]

The inescapable fact is that people have very different levels of comfort with technology and with changes in technologies they've become familiar with, whether you think they should be comfortable or not. They may also have powerful emotions about interacting with technologies, as anyone who's ever worked an IT help desk can tell you. This is both the opportunity and the peril.

The researcher Clifford Nass, a professor of communication at Stanford University and a pioneer of human-computer interaction studies, has made a specialty of diagnosing why people respond badly to new technologies. He reports in his book *The Man Who Lied to His Laptop* that male drivers in Germany were so annoyed by taking instructions from the female voice of BMW's GPS system that they flooded the customer service line with requests that the voice be changed. As Nass writes,

> The service desk received numerous calls from agitated German men that went something like this:
>
> CUSTOMER: I can't use my navigation system.
> OPERATOR: I'm very sorry about that sir. What seems to be the problem?
> CUSTOMER: A woman should not be giving directions.
> OPERATOR: Sir, it is not really a woman. It is only a recorded voice.
> CUSTOMER: I don't take directions from a woman.
> OPERATOR: Sir, if it makes you feel better, I am certain that the engineers that built the system and the cartographers who figured out the directions were all men.
> CUSTOMER: It doesn't matter. It simply doesn't work.[4]

Nass also explains that most people, however, prefer a female voice for computerized instructions, which is why Apple's Siri and Amtrak's automated Julie are both female voices. He theorizes that the female voice is generally more appealing because we hear our mother's voices first, while in the womb. That just goes to show how deeply rooted and emotionally tinged people's interactions with technology can be.[5]

The range of emotions evoked, or provoked, by the same product can be remarkable. Take, for example, the results of a study done to monitor how people would respond to a personal assistant robot in their homes.[6] The interviews people gave after living with the robots show fascinating differences in the ways they perceived and came to feel about the machines. Consider these two excerpts from the interview transcripts:

A

> I think I spoke to it occasionally, you know, because you feel sorry for this inanimate object, that is sort of programmed to speak and move. But that's all its [*sic*] doing. So I'd tell him sometimes where I was going and what I was doing, but I don't think it understood [laughs].

B

> It was just something in the way.... It was a bit of a nuisance really. I didn't find it really likeable. It was fairly uninteresting really, because its topics were limited and it was fairly, ehm, it was pretty much the same everyday [*sic*] and not very much on it. It was a bit boring really.

YOU'RE DESIGNING TO SERVE NEEDS

Users' degree of familiarity with new types of technologies and interfaces is only one key factor you have to always be thinking about. The different needs and desires of different types of users, as well as the different types of businesses and organizations you're designing for, must also be top of mind.

Teaching in New York City has exposed me to all kinds of industries I wouldn't normally have access to. It's one of the reasons I love it here over places like Silicon Valley. My students work in education, fashion, finance, sports, video games, television, music, and retail, not to mention other media outlets. All of these have particularities in terms of the functions that must be performed, the cultures of the companies, and the customers or audience they're serving. Needless to say, the goals of businesses in different industries vary widely. When I worked for the *Wall Street Journal*, a main goal for our app was to allow readers to get as much news of whatever kind they most wanted as quickly as possible. An app for an e-commerce site will have a main goal of driving people to hit the "Purchase" button. An app for a TV show will want to enhance the experience of watching the show in creative ways.

As for users, their needs and desires vary both by user and by the app or site. A younger Facebook user may resent ads on the site, while older users are desensitized to online ads from years of being marketed to and know how to ignore them. They might even appreciate some of the ads, if they're well tailored to the users' interests. The needs of a single user also change between sites. The same foodie user who goes onto Yelp looking for unvarnished customer critiques of restaurants is seeking very different information on the Food Network site, where spending some time with her favorite personalities is key.

Finding bridges between users' needs and your product's business goals is fundamental to UX design. The farther business goals deviate from user goals, the more care you will need to put into your design in order to satisfy both. Whether the bridge is a system feature, visual design, the copy you write, or an interaction or transition animation that you design into a product, the feelings users have as they cross each bridge combine to constitute the system's UX.

At the start of a project, you'll always be told the business objectives of your product and given a set of requirements for the features and services it should offer. But to truly please users, to create an optimal experience, you'll also need to carefully consider the context of who is using your product, when they started using it, how they access it, where they use it most often, and what their goals are. I ask these same questions whether I'm working on a small unpaid side project or for a behemoth media corporation.

That sounds great in principle, but until I actually started designing experiences, I always found it difficult to understand just how learning these things about users would change the way I'd design a product. So let me give a couple of specific examples.

One factor of users' lives you will want to consider is whether they're urban dwellers. Take the case of an app I often mention when I teach a class on mobile UX. The app used a service known as geofencing, which allows a mobile device to passively monitor where a user is through GPS. This app, which was called News.me (it no longer exists), used the service to request the location of a user's home. Then, when the user left home the app would wake up and automatically download new content. This made for a great experience for millions in New York City who have to wait on the subway platform on the way to work in the morning with no cell service. While they couldn't get updates for most of the apps on their phones during that time, News.me was loaded with new stories.

I highlight that this offline wait time in the subway is unique to urbanites. So does that make this feature meaningless for those who never take the subway? Not at all. All the users benefited from the absence of loading time. Which gets to a key point about the value of learning about users: one group's particular circumstances and needs can be fantastic leads for inspiration as to what features to offer, and often those features will have broad appeal for other users. Learning about differences among users doesn't mean that we'll necessarily create specific features tailored only to some users. Maybe you're working on a specialized app with a very targeted group of users, such as Lego fans or knitting enthusiasts, and you want to make your product highly specialized for them. But if you're working on a product with a broader base, you'll be more interested in probing into commonalities that even quite different users share, as we'll look into more later.

When I worked for the *Wall Street Journal* on the mobile app, we made a helpful observation about the ways different types of commuters used the app. Those who rode the bus to work interacted with the site much more, clicking on lots of stories, scrolling down through each section, saving stories, sharing them, and looking up stock quotes. Their hands and eyes were free to do so, whereas those who drove to work mostly used the feature that reads stories aloud for their commute time. This taught us that any new product we offered should include the audio service so those commuters could use it. But this discovery was also helpful because it led us to probe more into which features appealed to each type. We began to survey users, asking which features were "nice to have" and which they didn't much care about, and we found that both the bus riders and the drivers would appreciate a feature that would "publish" the paper for them at the time of day they woke up. This would give them the very latest news at that time. The fact that both sets of users wanted the feature led us to redesign some of the architecture of our publishing service, even though that involved a significant amount of time and money.

The people I design experiences for often surprise me. It happens as soon as I make an assumption about their behavior based on an anecdote I've heard about what they do or the way they are. Often, only after I see them interact with a site or app can I really see it through their eyes. Sometimes that's just too late; the product is finished. Which is why it's so important to do whatever you can to avail yourself of the methods that have been developed in UX to learn about users.

To make a design optimal, you've got to get to know how users are prepared to interact with your product, and you've got to understand what they want from it. You'll avoid many pitfalls, like wasting time on a feature no one really wants or pushing people to use a new technology they aren't ready for. I learned this lesson the hard way a few too many times. I fell into the classic trap of privileging what I wanted to do with an app or site over what would work best for my users.

WHEN PULL-TO-REFRESH ISN'T NATURAL

Working on the experience of WSJ Live, the *Wall Street Journal*'s iOS video app, I dug in for too long on my plan to make use of the pull-to-refresh feature that I loved about Twitter. The goal of the project I was working on was to make it easier for *Journal* readers to get through a lot of small video clips on the app. We were going to add a new feature that allowed readers to swipe to go to the next video, in addition to the old way of moving through them, which was by tapping a right-facing arrow button in the player controls. I loved that we were adding the feature because touch interactions are what the iPhone was made for. Not to use them was downright lazy on our part, I thought. But the trick was that touch interactions were new then, meaning I had to design the interaction so that it was empathetic as hell.

One potential problem was that people might perform the gesture accidentally and then be annoyed that the video had changed. I figured we could use the pull-to-refresh feature to prevent that, because it requires a purposeful swipe for about an inch across the screen as opposed to just an accidental flick of a few centimeters. Another thing that was appealing about using the feature was that it allows the user to perform the gesture anywhere on a page being viewed, and as the videos would be full-page view, this would make selecting the next easier; no button would be required for the user to call up the player controls. I figured, why not get rid of that outdated button method and use this new, proven technique, lifted right from one of my UX heroes, Loren Brichter, in the app he designed for Twitter? I'd just have to make the action work left to right, rather than vertically as it does with Twitter, because our videos scrolled horizontally.

The design was foolproof, in my mind. But there was still one issue I'd have to account for. Because the motion wasn't familiar for WSJ Live users, we'd need to alert them with a tip about how to use the new feature when they first opened the app. When I told a teammate my

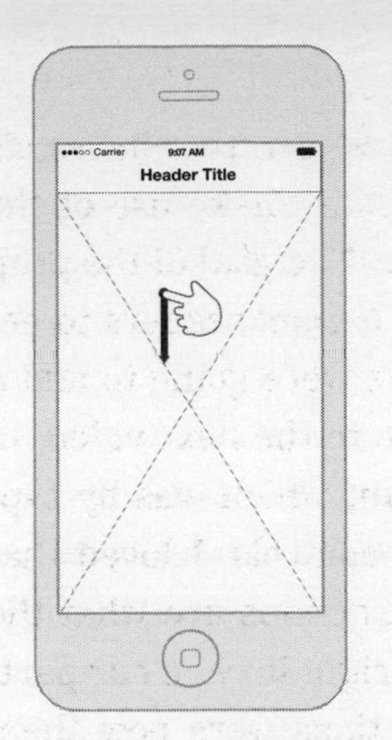

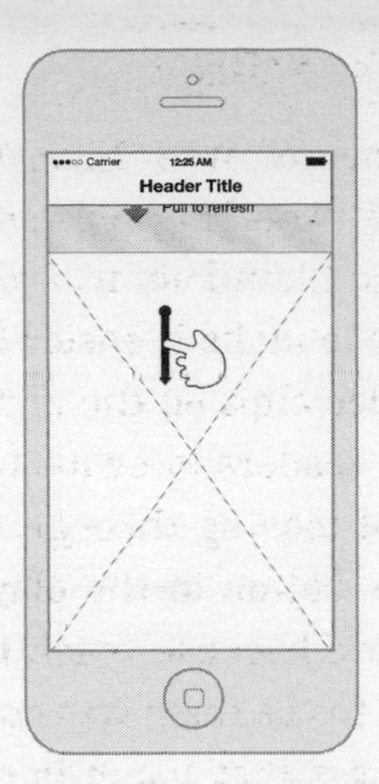

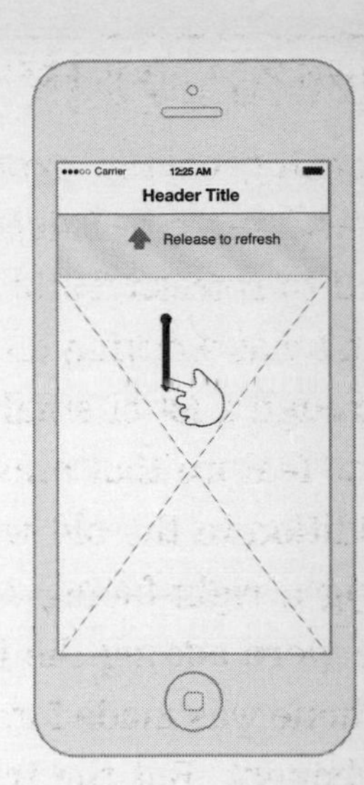

Left: Standard position, top of page. User begins dragging down. Middle: Pull-to-refresh area begins to appear. User is mid-gesture. Right: Pull-to-refresh area is in full view. User is ready to complete the gesture by releasing.

plan, she responded, "Don't make the interaction so complicated. Who cares if they mess up a few times?" She thought users would get used to the action quickly enough and that my design was over thought. "Who cares?!"

I responded. "I care!" I tried to explain the merits of my design, but the case wasn't being won, and before it got too out of hand (it was already slightly out of hand), I thought, "To the usability lab!" I figured that after a few tests I'd have all the ammunition of empirical user data I needed to back up my argument. Well, we didn't have a usability lab, so I did the next best thing. I got our developer to quickly program a prototype for an ad hoc user test that had a simple prompt—it would have to be simple to pass muster—and then asked some self-described video clip viewers among our less tech-savvy pool of coworkers to give it a try.

I prompted the test users with a brief statement of purpose before they opened the app: "Welcome to your updated app. We added a new feature to let you browse through videos faster. Open the app and try it out." Then, when they opened the app, a video started playing, as usual, but a tip appeared describing the new feature—"Swipe to go to the next video"—accompanied by an arrow showing the direction to swipe. After a few seconds, if the user hadn't swiped, the tip would disappear. I didn't see how it could fail.

Of the five people we tested, two of them missed the tip completely, one because he was distracted by something happening in the office and the other because he just outright dismissed it without reading it. Those two eventually found the feature, though, after playing around with the app a little, so I took heart. The other three all read the tip and then performed the swipe. Good results, right? Well, not so much. They had some confusion about how to do it at first and had some misfires. The key problem was that when they swiped, they did it too quickly and almost gingerly, which wasn't sufficient to activate the action. So as soon as they had completed their swipes, the video they'd already seen bounced back into position. That would totally irritate users.

Watching these test subjects taught me that the way I designed the system would have to be sensitive to the way users physically swiped as well as the way they naturally navigated through the app. Swiping, dragging, and flicking are actually very different interactions, and we have to design with an acute sensitivity to that.

As I thought about the design more, the nail in the coffin was when I realized why pull-to-refresh works naturally with the way Twitter users read tweets and didn't work naturally at all with the way WSJ Live users watched videos. It worked so well for Twitter readers because that app displays content vertically and in reverse chronological order, beginning with the tweets that have been posted since the last time the viewer opened the app. Viewers must swipe downward to scroll up through tweets toward the top to get to newer content, and when they reach the top, the same swipe action triggers the pull-to-refresh activation. If their swipe isn't vigorous enough to activate the refresh, their eyes have also been naturally drawn to the activation message "release to refresh" that appears at the top of the screen. And even if they don't see that at first—it's small and displays quickly—the repetitive dragging and flicking motion that Twitter users quickly learn is a behavior of discovery; they've been taught to interact with the app to find new material. So if they swipe down and no new content appears, it's like trying to turn the lights on when the power is out. Something is wrong. With the light switch, you naturally flip the switch at least once again, and Twitter users naturally swipe down again, more vigorously, which triggers the refresh. It's a brilliant design, which is why I was so hot to use it.

However, the experience of WSJ Live was quite different. We imagined users would let the app cycle through videos as if it were a TV. The video player was an unmoving interface element, unlike the scrollable list of tweets. Also, when people are watching a video, they focus on it, so when WSJ Live users were watching videos, their eyes wouldn't be naturally drawn to the right edge of the screen where the message "Pull to refresh" would have appeared, and there was no action they were familiar with on the app that would naturally draw their finger or eyes over there. I realized that most users would miss the pull-to-refresh message, never mind getting to the point where the message would switch to saying "Release to skip." Not only that, but to let users know what videos were available, we designed a menu to browse through that popped up on the screen when they clicked on a button. It was a horizontal list of video thumbnails, with the videos categorized into buckets such as politics, sports, and business. The new "swipe to skip" feature wouldn't pull up that menu.

My design hadn't taken into account how users would naturally be using the app or certain features we'd designed into it that they had become used to. I had made a classic UX design mistake: I was working backward from wanting to introduce a new feature, and I had assumed that readers would be annoyed by accidentally touching the screen and losing the video they were interested in watching. Good

UX is empathetic and always asks first, "Where is the user coming from?"

In the end we made it easier to complete the interaction and made sure the tip informing users of the new feature appeared the first time users opened the app and stayed up long enough to grab their attention. What we launched with wasn't perfect, and I can still think of ways to make it better, but it's now clear to WSJ Live users how to use it, and that was overridingly important.

WHAT IS UX, EXACTLY?

That experience with the WSJ Live app is a typical case in point of a project that a UX designer, or the person appointed to do UX design for a team, will be given. I hope that example begins to clarify the nature of the work and what's meant by *user experience*, which is a term that's been defined many ways and can be hard to wrap your head around. What, for the record, is the definition of user experience?

I'll defer to the two experts who've probably done the most to develop the field: Donald Norman, the famed product designer who was VP of research at Apple for years and who coined the term *user experience*, and Jakob Nielsen, who founded the discount usability engineering movement and was called "the guru of Web page usability" by the *New York Times*. On the website for the company they founded, Nielsen Norman Group, they write:

> "User experience" encompasses all aspects of the end-user's interaction with the company, its services, and its products.[7]

You can find lots of other definitions easily with a Google search, but I prefer this one because it's nice and simple and covers the full gamut. In this book, we're focusing on UX for web products, but the principles and techniques introduced apply across the board of product development.

A common misconception to dispel right away is that user experience really means usability. It's true that people often use the terms interchangeably, but usability is only one of the features of a product that contribute to the user experience. What are the other elements? A truly exhaustive list would be just about impossible to create, and, again, you'll find many variations. Usability is on every list, phrased in one way or another. Other key factors are the visual appeal of the graphic design and the emotional impact of the design. But for me, the most useful codification of the key things to be striving for in your designs is that formulated by Jakob Nielsen. He describes the essential components of a quality user experience as the following:

- **Learnability:** How easy is it for users to accomplish basic tasks the first time they encounter the design?
- **Efficiency:** Once users have learned the design, how quickly can they perform tasks?
- **Memorability:** When users return to the design after a period of not using it, how easily can they reestablish proficiency?
- **Errors:** How many errors do users make, how severe are these errors, and how easily can users recover from the errors?
- **Satisfaction:** How pleasant is it to use the design?[8]

I have drilled these into my brain, and I think about them every day, many times a day, as I work on designs. I even developed an acronym, which I pronounce "lemurs," that helps me remember them:

LEMErS

Type that up, print it out as large as you can, and pin it on your bulletin board. Turn to it every time you find yourself stuck about what to do with a design. If you are achieving these five key heuristics with your design, you are in very good shape. Then you can make your design more visually stunning and maybe add some cool bells and whistles to it.

So how do you determine whether your design is meeting these criteria? This is where UX design becomes a whole lot of fun.

GETTING TO KNOW YOUR USERS

The practice of UX design has come to encompass a long list of techniques for understanding users and their needs and desires and evaluating how you're serving them versus your competition. These include:

Use cases
User interviews
Stakeholder interviews
Surveys
Personas
Contextual inquiry
Content audit
Usability testing
Storyboarding
Diary studies
Competitor analysis
Analytics review

Different UX experts will advise different protocols for using these techniques and will have preferences among them. The truth is, though, that you're almost never going to be able to use all of these methods for one product within a single release cycle, not by a long shot, even if you're a UX specialist and that's your whole job. Typically you won't have either the time or the money. If you're a part-time UX specialist, you'll likely be brought in just to make sure there are no confusing moments for users when interacting with the product, to ensure that the best options for user interface (UI) are chosen, and to talk through the use cases that your design addresses. Use cases are descriptions of the ways that users will perform specific tasks on your product, such as searching or purchasing. If you're an engineer at a startup or small company, you'll probably just be trying to get some UX design in in the midst of juggling all the other work you've got to be doing.

So I advise that at the start, for learning about your users, you focus on doing interviews and surveys and then creating personas. This is a good core empathetic design tool kit, and this process should be thought of as necessary to understanding how people will interact with your site or app and try to perform any given task. As you progress, you can learn more and more techniques and try to find opportunities to apply them, or come up with your own simple variations on them.

Creating Portraits of Your Users

Personas are representative descriptions of your users that you create based on data collected in your surveys and interviews. If you're working on an existing product, or one to serve the users of another product your company offers, you can also find some valuable information for personas in your product's or company's usage statistics, such as how many and of what profile access one particular part of the product versus another. Personas cover specifics of behaviors, such as commuting, exercising, mobile use, or what users find entertaining; general demographics, such as income, age, familiarity with technology, location, and occupation; and scenarios common to the user base, such as searching for an item to compare prices, watching a TV series, or tracking how much meat one eats.

If I had taken the time to make up detailed personas for the WSJ Live app, I would have learned sooner the ways users interacted with the video content, the other apps they might have been exposed to, and the times they'd be most likely to engage with the product. My mistake was making an app for someone too much like me.

I don't know about you, but when I think of a *Wall Street Journal* user, here's who I *don't* think of: a twentysomething freshly moved to Brooklyn with upward of $30,000 in student loan debt. His daily routine begins with rolling out of bed around eight thirty to check his iPhone for any missed texts or alerts from the staggering number of apps he's downloaded. Afterward he moseys down to the local cafe for some iced coffee because it's summer and the air conditioner is on the fritz. Upon returning to his apartment he hops on his Apple MacBook Pro and begins browsing through Twitter to see what's been happening in the worlds of tech, science, food, music, and design. Checking email is also part of his morning routine, but there's typically not much to respond to because at this time of day the only new emails are from daily deal sites. After that, he heads into Manhattan on bike to stalk coworking spaces and hunt for startup jobs.

What I just described was me fresh out of college, and I was very much not the audience I was designing for. I learned the value of personas to quickly tell the story of an actual user. I've found they are very useful in helping me to keep focus on the user, rather than getting caught up in some feature I've become infatuated by. They aid in thinking through the different scenarios that people are using my products in and then conjuring up ideas about ways I can make their day better. Personas transform users from abstract entities into vivid, multidimensional beings.

So what makes for a really useful persona? There are many formats used, and you can find lots of examples and templates on the web. But here is one I use that gives you a feel for a good format to use and the level of specificity to aim for. I find it's important to include a photograph, and you can either take one of a colleague or friend who fits the persona or find one online among the wealth of photographs posted.

When I joined the *Wall Street Journal* several personas had already been created. We knew that readers liked to talk about what section a story appeared in and that many of them liked to read every single story each day. One reason for this is the social capital in being able to say they read the story that appeared on B1—the first page of the Business and Finance section—in the *Journal* that morning. Knowing this led us to structure content in the iPhone app according to the sections of the paper and in a way that allowed users to quickly scan through all stories in the sections. Specifically, we made sure that whenever an image accompanied a story, the image would be right-aligned in the list of articles (represented by the box with an X through it in the

Max
Persona for a social photo taking app.

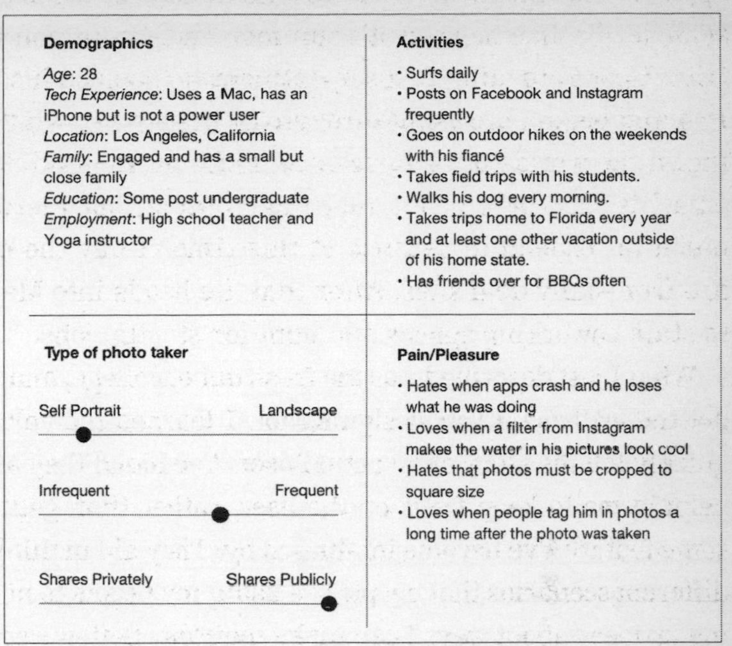

Demographics
Age: 28
Tech Experience: Uses a Mac, has an iPhone but is not a power user
Location: Los Angeles, California
Family: Engaged and has a small but close family
Education: Some post undergraduate
Employment: High school teacher and Yoga instructor
Activities
• Surfs daily
• Posts on Facebook and Instagram frequently
• Goes on outdoor hikes on the weekends with his fiancé
• Takes field trips with his students.
• Walks his dog every morning.
• Takes trips home to Florida every year and at least one other vacation outside of his home state.
• Has friends over for BBQs often
Type of photo taker
Self Portrait
Landscape
Infrequent
Frequent
Shares Privately
Shares Publicly
Pain/Pleasure
• Hates when apps crash and he loses what he was doing
• Loves when a filter from Instagram makes the water in his pictures look cool
• Hates that photos must be cropped to square size
• Loves when people tag him in photos a long time after the photo was taken

A persona detailing characteristics to help humanize a hypothetical target user. Their main function is to prevent citing our own qualities as representative of the user base. Personas get a bad rap when used to describe affective parts of users but when behaviors are in focus, their true value shines.

next figure) with the title of the article wrapping around the image, rather than the titles being left-aligned and the images being scattered in different spots. The result is a steady line that the user's eye is able to travel down in order to more efficiently scan headlines.

One of your main goals in creating a persona is always to get a good description of the majority of the user base. This can be tricky because for some sites and apps, users vary widely. For example, I work on three mobile products at Yahoo—Finance, Screen, and Entertainment. For Yahoo Finance some of our users are interested in finance and economic data only, while others are general news

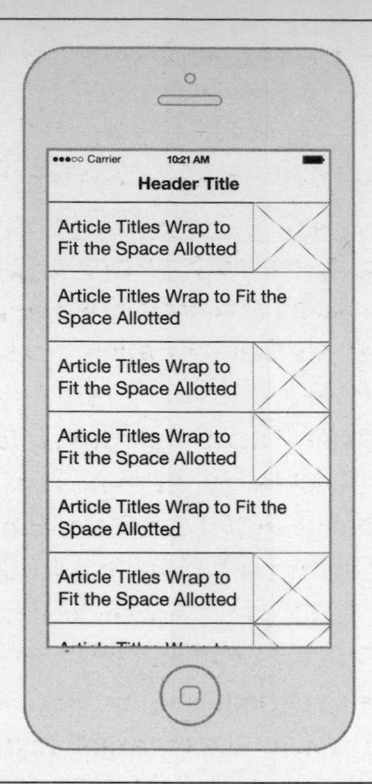

Right-aligned images allow users to scan quickly down the left edge of the screen even when no image is present. This applies to both mobile and desktop.

junkies. Some follow Asian markets from the U.S. and some don't care what happens outside of the one or two tech companies they invest in. When creating your personas, you aren't looking at first for those more rarefied interests. You want to start by finding the overlaps in users' problems and goals and the ways they currently solve them. You're looking for trends in behavior that stretch across large swaths of the user base. It's important to cover the big stuff before getting to the idiosyncrasies of specific personas. Eventually you might want to create several different personas to capture those nuances.

Personas are great for helping teams play out scenarios of how products will be used and how they could be improved, and they're especially helpful for picking what to work on first and how much time to spend designing and developing to ensure that the feature meets the level of polish that users will expect. They are also a great way to prioritize features your users want over those you'd love to give them. Doing the work of creating personas helps you pick up on changes in user behavior and interests that may allow you to tailor your design in important ways.

For example, before 2011 most *Wall Street Journal* users accessed our mobile sites on a BlackBerry. In some areas that's still true, but the trend started to change in 2011 for European users. Data collected through web tracking software told us that in Germany, iPhones and Androids had become the leading devices our users viewed us on. So when we began designing the German-language mobile website for one of the *Journal*'s specialty periodicals, the *CFO Journal*, we decided to forgo the extra time it would take to target anything but Android and iPhone devices. Not having to design within the constraints of the BlackBerry meant one less screen size to optimize for and one less interaction to design for; we didn't need to worry about the BlackBerry's unique trackball and keyboard. (Mind you, though, that didn't mean I designed all kinds of new features especially for the new devices' particular capabilities. Just because a device can do something doesn't mean someone will make use of it. So you still want to base your designs on user behavior more than the capabilities of a device.)

The key ways to get the richness of user description you want are interviews and surveys, and I recommend that you do at least some of both. There are issues with both methods, but the common pitfalls are easy enough to avoid if you know what they are.

A Little Listening Goes a Long Way

When I sit down to conduct an interview I start by asking how the interviewee's day is going. I want to know what kind of state they are in and if there is anything I can do to make them more comfortable. My interview subjects come from different sources. They may be friends of coworkers or recruited subjects who have gone through a screening process. Interview questions should revolve around issues of content, activities, feelings, and the settings in which a product is used.

An appropriate interview question for developing a persona for a video app would seek to understand what television programs a user enjoys. Taking a look at those programs would be a way to gather some good data about what users will like. If my users overwhelmingly enjoy *SportsCenter* on ESPN, then I might want to structure my interface in a way that's similar to the way *SportsCenter* lists the upcoming topics and the amount of time that will be spent on each one along the side of the screen. If my users were all *Star Trek* fans, then the design would probably look a lot like LCARS. (For those who aren't Trekkies, LCARS is the screen display on the computers on the starship *Enterprise*.)

I like to be colloquial and have fun with the person I am interviewing, because allowing the process to be more friendly and free-form tends to reveal more, including things I'd never have thought to ask about. I once got sidetracked talking about the Mets for ten minutes in an interview and learned that my interviewee had an app solely dedicated to Mets news. In all the interviews that followed I made sure to ask about any such specialty apps and sites users were fans of. One of the best benefits of interviewing is hearing about the different scenarios an interviewee goes through in her daily routine, regardless of the interactions she has with the product you're designing for, which can provide great ideas for new features to offer. You might learn that many of your users are encountering bad traffic on their way to work and decide to include a traffic update feature in your app. Or maybe you're working on a grocery e-commerce site and discover that quite a few of your users are dieting, so you decide to add a calorie counter feature.

Once you've explored users' interests and daily activities more generally this way, you can start to ask more specific questions about how they interact with your product, or, if your product is still in development, how they interact with a prototype or with related products that you can show them on-screen as you talk. You want to ask questions such as:

- When do you use the app?
- Can you show me how you go through the tasks you usually perform?
- Which devices do you access the app on?
- How do you do [a certain task]?
- Where would you start?
- What would you do next?
- What information do you need to complete this task?
- Can you show me how you do that?
- Is any part of this process difficult or frustrating?
- Is that what you were hoping for?
- What's the most enjoyable part of this process for you?

When I was with the *Journal*, collecting information about how users felt about the competition, such as CNN and the *New York Times*, was also central to my interview process. If you give a user something familiar to critique or respond to, you spend less time leading the conversation and letting them do more of the talking, and their responses about competitors can be very useful in determining dos and don'ts.

After the series of interviews is over the results should be tallied to determine whether behaviors are confined to a small set of users or are true of many users. The idea is to find trends across interviews so the design addresses issues faced by the majority. So, for example, you might find that some key group of users is by far most interested in checking the Dow Jones ticker when they log on to your app, but most users want to see a good range of top stories. To cater to the smaller group, you'd put a link to the ticker, for sure, or maybe even give a small version of it on the home page, but you wouldn't make it the most prominent feature. Maybe that also tells you, though, that there would be a good user base for a specialized app that's more specifically about checking the very latest of-the-moment financial data.

Interviews can get expensive, but that drawback can be solved by conducting them around one's own workplace and with friends. Really, any feedback you can get will be helpful. I heard a story about a guy who had a sign outside a coffee shop that read COFFEE IS ON JIM FOR 5 SECONDS OF YOUR TIME. In that short amount of time you can ask people one question to gauge interest in an idea or gather stats on competing services (e.g., who does it better), or show them a design for a moment and then have them tell you what they remember. Any amount of time with a real user is better than none.

One important thing I've learned to remember with interviewing is that I may influence how people answer my questions. While digging deeper into a response that interests me is a great way to get richer feedback, I may also be biasing them with leading questions. For example, if I ask, "Do you find the purchasing process too complicated?" they're likely to say they do. People have a subconscious desire to want to help you make your case and give you the information you're hoping for.

This is one reason that it's good to also take surveys.

Sending Out Surveys

Surveys aren't subject to going off on tangents; they provide a useful complement to the interview process because they're less likely to bias users' answers. They can also be more cost effective and farther reaching than interviews. They can even generate enough data to create good personas on their own.

A key guideline for creating a survey is to make it easy to take. It's funny how much UX applies to the practice of itself. A difficult-to-use survey will lead to drop-offs. What makes a survey difficult is the same thing that makes an experience bad: making the user think too much. Use clear, short, and specific sentences to avoid encumbering users.

You also want to make the survey quick to take. It should not have too many questions and shouldn't require the taker to reach back too far in memory. I would not be able to tell you how much online shopping I've done in the past six months, for example, but I can tell you I didn't do any today, and that the last thing I bought was not online but I used the store's mobile website while I was there to find what I was looking for.

Another way I've found to keep people from getting frustrated with my surveys is to use proper entry methods for each field of the form. Radio buttons offering multiple choice answers are especially effective, but they must have proper instructions letting users know when they need to pick one thing and when they should select all the items that might apply. Another good practice is using the numerical keyboard on mobile devices for form fields that require numerical responses. However you design a survey, an overriding imperative is that users can move quickly through it.

Two things I particularly like to do in surveys in order to keep the user's attention are to use image-based questions (for example, showing the screenshot of the feature I'm asking about or three versions of an interface I'm working on) and to have branches of follow-up questions based on responses. It's also good to start by branching users off according to the device they use. If a user answers that they own an Android device, for example, the remaining questions and answer options should contain Android-centric language.

One golden rule of survey creation is to take the survey yourself before sending it out. I also send my surveys to other team members so they can help me look for errors or refine the language. Not reviewing the language of the survey yourself or with others is one of the most common mistakes my students make.

THE INTERESTS OF STAKEHOLDERS

There's one other group of people you're going to need to understand in order to create the best product: the people who approve your design. Typically this isn't just your product manager or whatever boss you're reporting to; there are multiple stakeholders, and they represent different perspectives and interests within the team and company, from marketing and sales to the business team keeping track of costs and the engineering team, with their own issues regarding time and systems capabilities. You can come up with the most wildly appealing experience design for users but see your work go for naught if the stakeholders don't approve it.

As frustrating as the process of getting approval from all parties can be, you'll find over time that they can give you profound ways of rethinking your design. And you always have to be prepared for criticisms; most assuredly some stakeholders won't accept your recommendations. Their decision to reject your design ideas may be influenced by external pressures, such as the launch date of a competitive product, or may be for internal reasons, such as how busy the engineering team is with other projects, or may just be based on their own biases. What matters most in bringing them around, I've found, is persuasive insistence. Defending the experience of our users is what we are paid to do, whether the people who've hired us know it or not. We've got to be diplomatic, respectful, and responsive to stakeholders' input. And there are many times when we should take their advice and make changes, which I will cover much more fully later on, when we discuss creating prototypes and presenting ideas. But as this chapter focuses on the mandate to serve user needs, for now I want to emphasize the importance of sometimes holding firm and of finding persuasive ways to make your case.

One of my biggest failures while designing for the *Wall Street Journal* concerned a feature of the redesign of our flagship app for the iPhone, one of the biggest projects I worked on for the *Journal*. This was the flagship app for a device that dominated our user base, and I knew we would be launching with a feature that would decimate our four-and-a-half-star App Store rating.

The app for the iPad was designed to look like a newspaper and operate with the same natural user interface of the paper columns of text across the page.

Our redesign was going to make the app into a universal iOS app, meaning the same code base would be used for both iPhone and iPad. Any difference in the core architecture would mean branching the code and making the app larger and harder to maintain, which of

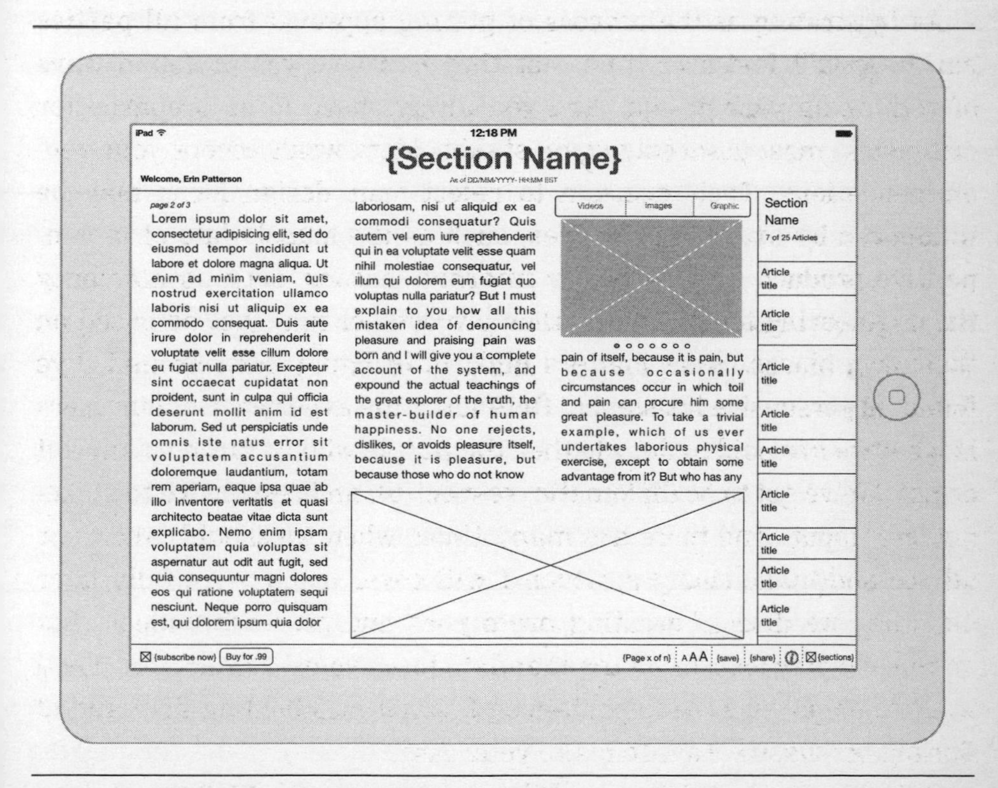

WSJ Live iPad app article continuation page

course would involve more time and money. Nonetheless, I was going to recommend just that: creating a different architecture for the phone app. I wanted to change the way article pages worked from horizontal on the iPad to vertical just for iPhone.

On the iPad, the horizontal swipe to advance to the next page feels natural because the page looks more like that of a magazine than a newspaper, and the swiping action is an intuitive approximation of turning the page. But on the iPhone we wouldn't get the same amount of space. A one-column vertical layout is the standard; anything else looks cramped and users usually have to expand the size of the text in order to be able to read it. Therein lay the problem—our code stated that pages were organized horizontally, and to change that meant more development time would be needed.

This was even more perverse to my mind because the current app we were replacing used a single vertical page, as did our mobile website. All our competitors in the news space on both native and mobile web used the vertical smooth scrolling page. The only instances of horizontal pagination among competitors were on Kindle for iPhone, the iBooks app, and the read-it-later bookmarking app Instapaper. But to use these as design defense for horizontal pagination in our iPhone app meant ignoring the facts about the nature of the content. Kindle and iBooks were meant to house long-form content like books, while Instapaper is meant for content that is too long to get through at the moment; it saves the content for you to read later and offers the option to read it on another device, which suggests that one orientation is not better than the other.

The arguments I made weren't enough, though. My boss wasn't convinced that the impact on our timeline was not worth the effort. I could have stood my ground and emphasized the data more, the fact that our personas and the information we had about how users navigated through our current app supported the vertical scroll design and that none of our competitors were penalizing users for moving between platforms, as the horizontal design would do. Instead I built two prototypes to put in the hands of my stakeholders. The idea was to give my boss, in particular, the experience of confusion in reading articles in the hope that he'd realize the mistake. But instead he latched on to the design and made himself think it wasn't so bad and that he, and all other users, could get used to it.

The point fell flat, and I'd spent a good deal of time trying to make the prototype interactive and as high-fidelity as possible. I was using the wrong methods to speak to my stakeholder. If I could go back now I'd do it all differently. I'd mock up only the first page, put it on a phone, and walk through the office tallying how many people said they would swipe vertically to move through the article. Such a simple, low-cost test carried out the moment the issue came up would probably have been sufficient to make the case for extending our deadline. I took too long to build a complex prototype to test something that already had great evidence in its favor. Worst of all, though, the prototype gave credence to the alternate possibility.

That experience taught me a lesson I'll always be reminding myself about—pick your battles and how you'll fight them. I had fought for other design features of the app, but this was the most important one, core to the experience. I should have better anticipated how dug in my boss was going to be about the timeline—as bosses very often are—and gathered more support before going to him, and I should have worked more quickly. I also should never have shown him such a fully developed prototype in order to make a basic point about such a fundamental aspect of utility.

DESIGN FOR CORE USER'S NEEDS

With your business requirements, personas, and user data in hand, you've got a good set of basic insights for making choices about what interfaces to use given the context of your users, their goals, and whether those goals deviate from the business goals. As you begin crafting your design, there is an additional set of factors you want to focus on, which I'll discuss throughout the course of the book. For now, I'll focus on two of them, the first two of Nielsen's LEMErS: learnability and efficiency.

When I am in the thick of designing an interface and considering the possible features to include, I often ask myself: Do my users need to learn anything here? How essential is this feature I'm thinking of using? Does anyone care about learning some new feature, especially if it is secondary to the thing they are trying to accomplish?

With the WSJ Live video app, we were told we had significant constraints on how many changes to the community's habits we should force, because those habits were deeply ingrained. There's a way they like to watch the news, and it was important that we didn't interfere with that. For users who have daily habits, like watching TV news, learning a new way to consume the same old content is just not at the forefront of needs. That said, we decided that using the new swipe technology for video viewing was an important value-add that they would appreciate. So the requirement that they learn how to do it was acceptable, in large part because we knew it was a really quick learning process. But we still worked to make the process as smooth as possible.

When it came to the *Journal*'s flagship news app, because of the decision to go with the multiple columns across the page format, we had to educate the user that the articles continued after that first page. At the bottom of the first page of each article, we had to add an indicator: ARTICLE CONTINUES →. This should have been seen as blunt proof that we had the wrong interface. You always want to do as little teaching as necessary.

PRIVILEGE THE USER'S GOALS

Looking back to my experiences at the *Journal*, one of the most important things I learned was not to get in the way of my user's goal. The pull I felt to introduce new features was particularly strong in regard to my desire to harness the capabilities of the iPad's touch interface. I wanted to perfect our gesture-based navigation and get rid of our clunky buttons.

The app was made up of a mix of natural user interface (NUI) elements and graphical user interface (GUI) ones. Users could move between sections of the app by swiping down, which was a fairly close approximation of the natural movement of reading a physical newspaper, reading top to bottom down the columns. But they could also choose to navigate with a graphical interface, which was a button on the bottom of the app labeled "Sections" that, when tapped, would give users a menu. I was designing for a touch interface, so I figured we should be redesigning substantially to embrace that—I wanted to do away with the buttons. But I was told to avoid introducing new types of interactions and stick to familiar, persistent on-screen interface elements.

My boss's position was that it would be too risky to rely solely on the gestures that a touch screen interface affords and that a whole new educational walkthrough on how to use the app would be required. I agreed that removing buttons would mean having to educate our users on the gestural interactions, but I knew there were other means besides overt tips and walkthroughs to educate a user. The concept of showing instead of telling users how to work a new feature is growing in popularity now, but it was completely new then, and my boss wasn't buying it. Her resistance came from the other key factor I'm emphasizing here: efficiency. You always want to make repetitive tasks as quick and simple as possible for users. It's a valid point that bears repeating—don't get in the way.

PRIVILEGE THE USER'S TIME

It's important to put people through as few steps as possible to get to the things they want, be those steps solely cognitive or ones that require a physical interaction. It's enough that users are likely already dealing with a new type of device, as we're all now constantly doing. Adding any more time to their experience is a fundamental source of irritation. Stop and really think about requiring them to reverse the way they scroll or removing clues to interactivity, like hover states. Those are significant changes that can really confuse users.

This is why I remove as much educational interface up front as I can. All users should be able to comfortably view the content that goes into the products I work on, whether for the *Journal* or for Yahoo. Their core interest is in the article, image, or video page, not in supplementary features of the product. Many sites and apps are guilty of presenting users with too much to learn.

The interactions that my users can or must perform need to be as dead simple and obvious as possible. Things like text resizing, volume adjustment, and the option to look at an image in a full-screen view should be either blatantly obvious or designed and tested to find the right default. Learning how to do something on a site or app should never feel like an exercise.

THERE IS NOTHING WRONG WITH THE FAMILIAR

One of the best ways to make sure you're not overtaxing your users' interest in learning new ways to navigate is to use established design patterns. Here's a design pattern I'm sure you're familiar with: Where does the search box on most content and retail sites live? Most of the page is taken up by articles or by product images and offers. The navigation is at the top or maybe on the left. So where would you find search? Hopefully you answered top right. Even in the Mac operating system, the search tool is placed there.

Design patterns shouldn't be thought of as hard and fast rules; they are guidelines, and sometimes there are good reasons to deviate from them. A good example of deviating from the search pattern would be a search engine, like Google or Bing, where the main purpose of the site is search. Then the best placement is most likely dead center. So even something as universal as search, whose design pattern holds generally across the web, breaks the rules when the context necessitates.

Another design pattern, which is rapidly gaining in popularity, was introduced by Facebook in October 2011 to its mobile apps and websites. It's known as the hamburger button: three horizontal lines that resemble (sort of) two buns and a patty. This button takes users to a menu underneath the main screen. I used the same pattern when designing the *Wall Street Journal*'s iPhone app and mobile website. On one of the last projects I worked on for the *Journal*, an editor involved in the design process was intent on having a button labeled "menu" next to the hamburger because he was not a mobile Facebook user. He didn't think the hamburger was familiar enough. In the end the design team got the final say, largely due to how many other apps we showed were using it, including one of our own. The button was deemed easily learnable not only because so many of our users were already familiar with it from our own app, but also because of the large overlap we shared with the Facebook user base. Interestingly enough, Facebook has moved away from this pattern because the hidden menu items prove too large a barrier to the level of engagement Facebook is interested in across its very large and very diverse user base. Facebook restored its tabbed interface to keep users aware of the sections most used in the app: news feed, messages, notifications, and requests.

Exactly how is a design pattern defined? It is a trend in the placement, aesthetic treatment, or interactivity of a feature. Some design patterns become so familiar that they are expected and users can be annoyed if they're not available—like scrolling up through an article page on an iPhone! And remember, you never want to underestimate the dissatisfaction caused by bucking familiarity. Trying to follow what is most familiar for users of different devices can get tricky, even for people like me who do this for a living. I use an iPhone for my personal calls and an Android for work matters. I can't tell you the number of times I've tried to swipe to delete something—an iOS feature—on my Android phone.

But the love of familiarity doesn't mean you can't play around a little with a design pattern. In fact, that can be a great way to innovate a better solution for your particular product. Both Apple and Facebook made a modification to the Twitter pull-to-refresh design that I found interesting—not because it was more innovative but because it showcased the power of design patterns. Both the iOS Mail app and Facebook position users at the top of their feeds of content at the outset, and again each time the feed is refreshed. This is different from Twitter, which positions users at the bottom of the list with the oldest content. Although seemingly small, this difference does result in a different flow with users swiping up to go down the list through new content before reaching old content and vice versa. Twitter had the onus of introducing this new interaction to users and thus needed to make it learnable. They did so by letting the users discover it by putting it right in their path; the same interaction accomplishes both navigation and refreshing—in iOS Mail and Facebook there are two separate interactions.

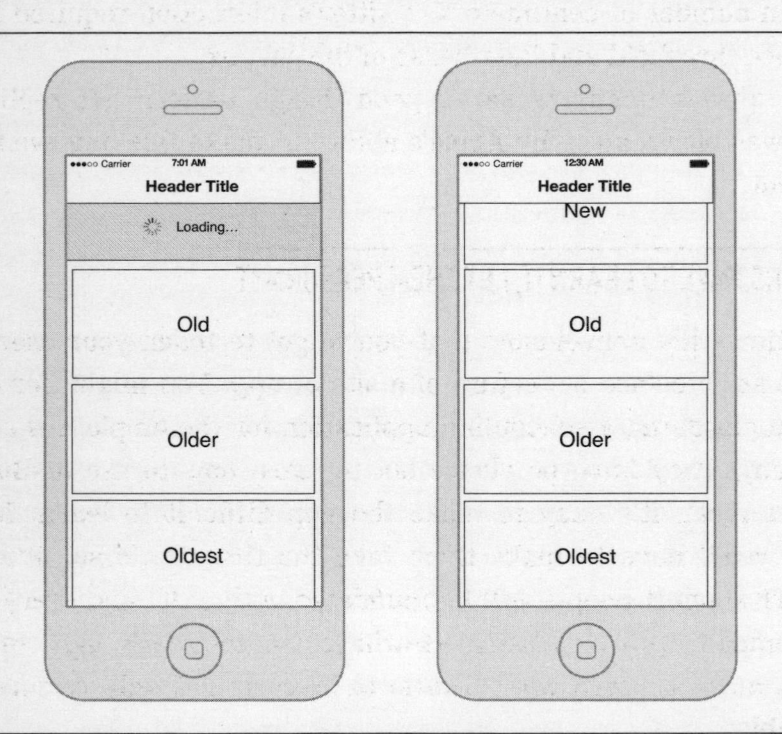

Left: Updating state for a reverse-chronologically ordered feed. The user has reached the end of the feed of new content. Right: After update is completed the user can see what is old content and what is new, reducing recall.

Why would Facebook and Apple use the pull-to-refresh at the top of the feed even though their users begin at the top of the list and move down, away from the thing they will need once they get to the end of the list? Why do they use the pull-to-refresh at all? Because the design pattern exemplifies the usability LEMErS of efficiency and learnability so well it is a natural solution. There was a flexibility and efficiency of use that sped up how a user would interact with the touch interface. A vertical swiping gesture was used for both navigation and refreshing. This also meant a minimalist design because there was no need for a refresh button on the interface. And Apple actually improved on the interaction by triggering the refresh after a certain distance threshold is reached. This means you trigger the action by dragging a certain number of centimeters. Twitter's interaction required both a distance threshold and the release of the gesture.

I'm always happy to see a good design pattern get replicated, but I was blown away by Apple's ability to make this one even more efficient.

IF USERS HAVE TO LEARN IT, LET THEM PERFORM IT

Sometimes it's unavoidable that you've got to teach your users how to use an interface or feature of a site or app. You might, for example, be designing a scheduling application for the employees at your company. They have no choice but to learn how to use it. But that doesn't mean it's okay to make the app difficult to learn. It does mean you'll have to make them take the time to do so; otherwise your IT support people will be inundated with calls and everyone at the company will be frustrated, which can get really ugly. In some cases, making users work a little to learn is not only required but desirable.

When this is the case, try hard not to resort to the common solution of using an overlay to point out what each interface element does. A lot of sites and apps are guilty of presenting users with too much to learn all at once this way. UX designers should question whether they need to have any such overlay at all. As one of the designers I've had the pleasure of working with likes to say, "If you need to describe your interface, you have a bad interface." You should look hard for other solutions.

A great way to make things easily learnable is to make the action of learning a performative experience. Video games engage their users—we all know that—and one of the things they are great at is teaching people how to play them. If they weren't, they'd have a pretty big usability problem on their hands. The way they teach people is by having them perform the actions they will be using throughout the game. Often the game introduces one action at a time, such as in Cut the Rope, a popular mobile puzzle game for iPhone, Android, and other emerging gestural interfaces like the Leap Motion, which detects gestures in the air. The object of each puzzle is to feed a little guy on-screen. With each progressive stage the puzzles get harder, requiring you to perform more and more advanced gesture combinations and sequences. But the first one shows the food dangling on a piece of rope with text saying "Slide your finger to cut the rope" next to a drawing of a finger with a dotted line crossing the rope. The little guy sits patiently, pleading for you to act by occasionally pointing into his open mouth to indicate his hunger. The interface just waits for you to interact, making you learn how to play before allowing you to advance.

Another good example of a performative learning experience can be found in the to-do list app Clear. If you don't have the app, put this book down now, download it, and go through the experience. Granted, it has a walkthrough at first (at least in version 1.2.2), but after the introduction you are prompted with a to-do list. Think of that, a to-do list in a to-do list app—makes perfect sense.

But you may be thinking, *Why do I need to learn how to write a to-do list? How simple is that?* Clear is trying to get users accustomed to making their lists with the touch interface. The interesting thing about a touch interface is that the whole thing is interactive, and it allows many different types of interactions. You can swipe on it at different speeds; you can tap, double tap, or even triple tap; and it doesn't end there. The only difficult thing about this new type of interface is its newness, which means not many people are used to it right now. So Clear has its users perform each of the actions the app allows, one at a time.

The first list item says, "Swipe to the right to complete!" When you do this, the item you've completed is struck through; the color behind it changes briefly from red, which is the background color for active list items, to green; and a check mark briefly appears. When you release your swipe gesture from the screen to complete the action, the phone vibrates and the finished item moves to the bottom of the list and becomes grayed out (so you can still see the items you've crossed out). If you cross out an item by mistake, all you have to do is swipe to the left on the now-crossed-out item and it is reinstated (you learn this in the to-do list tutorial, too).

The only change I'd be interested in testing would be to make the text read "Swipe me to the right!," deleting "to complete."

I would add the word *me* in order to personify the command and create a deeper connection with the user. Ideally we want the dialogue between a system and the person using it to be as rich as those we have in the real world. I would delete "to complete" because I think performing the action makes what it does so obvious that you don't really need to spell it out.

Learnability integrated as content in this way tests well with the users I've studied. This may not be an option, though, and if no other alternative than an overlay is available, the lesson from video games can still be applied. Instead of saying everything at once, show users functionality that might be somewhat new or unfamiliar when they express a desire or need for it. For example, if the business I work for wants to educate its employees to become more efficient with their computers by learning keyboard shortcuts, I would write a program that required users to try to find the right shortcut several times within a certain period of time before they would be shown an overlaid tip with the corresponding key command.

THE GIFT OF CONSTRAINTS

This chapter has given you a first basic set of guidelines for being responsive to users' needs in your designs. These guidelines have been focused on the constraints involved with users' familiarity with the features you'd like to design into your product and with the business's mandates in terms of time, money, and novelty. But there is another fundamental set of constraints that UX designers should become intimately aware of and learn as much about as they practically can, which are the constraints of the system you've got to work with.

Back-end systems creators and front-end interface creators can seem to be working in separate worlds. The push and pull between back and front end is endemic in web development. You could say it's built into the system. But I have found that developing a good understanding of the system I'm designing for and its constraints has not only saved me a great deal of time and frustration, but actually helped me create better designs. That's the subject we'll turn to next.

POINTS TO REMEMBER

Seeing Through Users' Eyes:

» Never underestimate how differently various users will respond to a design; the way they interact with your site or app will depend on a wide range of factors, from their age to where they live and their life situations. Your first job is understanding the full range of your users.

» Finding bridges between users' needs and desires and those of the business is vital; and the more business and user goals diverge, the more thought you must put into your design.

- Always consider the context in which users will engage with the product; this can lead to important ideas for features to add and ways to tailor your design.
- User experience does not mean simply usability; usability is only one of the core elements of UX. Always keep the LEMErS in mind: learnability, efficiency, memorability, errors, and satisfaction.
- Doing user interviews and surveys and then creating personas is a good core tool kit for user research, and these should be done for every project.
- In conducting interviews, be personable and don't lead the witness. Start off in a friendly way and get to know a little about the interviewee before diving into your questions. This will lead to ideas for unexpected questions.
- There is nothing wrong with the familiar; always consider which design patterns you should make use of.
- If users have to learn about a feature or gesture, let them perform it. Build learning into your design.

Chapter 2

CREATIVITY LOVES CONSTRAINTS

A good friend of mine, Erin Sparling, is one of the most ingenious people I've met when it comes to technology. He's always finding new things to hook up to the web, like the time he connected the front door of his apartment to Foursquare. He programmed the door to unlock when a friend comes over and checks in with the Foursquare app. He's built a coffee table that doubles as a web server and has connected various appliances to the web and programmed them to turn on when he sends a signal. I've asked him to lecture about technology in all the classes I've taught at General Assembly, and he never ceases to impress with his ninja presentation skills.

He calls the talk that he gives "Boundary Conditions of an Arbitrary Medium." I love this lecture because it covers one of the most important questions that UX designers are always grappling with: What are the constraints and capabilities of the system we're designing for? In web design, new technological developments are always coming along, and we've got to consider whether they're appropriate for any given project. But we're also always facing constraints that mean some of the things we'd love to make a site or app do just aren't possible, or at least not yet.

Erin uses the progression of technology in oil paints to illustrate how the repertoire of current technologies has so much to do with shaping any project. He shows how during the Renaissance and up to the late 1800s, artists had to make their paints from various sources of pigment, like lapis lazuli, which they'd grind into a powder, and some form of binding agent, like tree gum or egg yolk. Paint had to be prepared fresh for every painting session, and this made portability a problem, confining painters largely indoors. Eventually, painting was able to move from the studio to the outdoors with the invention of the metal paint tube. Before long, the impressionist painters were breaking the boundaries of the form with their masterworks capturing the delicate dance of sunlight glistening over seascapes and animating haystacks with an early-morning glow.

Probably no domain of human creativity has been tied so closely to technological advances as design in computing, and the pace has been staggering. I'm often working with video, and given the state of the art now, it's amazing to recall that up until 2009, none of the browser vendors had settled on a video format standard. That forced developers to encode multiple versions of any web-embedded video, which was a real slog. Apple and Microsoft solved this by pushing through the h.264 standard, and video online has boomed. Now we're in the throes of the shift to mobile, and we've got to be totally up to speed with responsive design, geolocation, voice commands, and touch interactions. But as fast as changes evolve in computing, they're also always incremental. When phones first went mobile, they were fundamentally like landline phones, with large keypads, and they were only voice enabled. They were also about the size of a brick and almost as heavy.

The phone that's widely considered the first smartphone, the IBM Simon, wasn't invented until twenty years later, and it showcased a retinue of new features, such as a pager, a fax machine, and a personal digital assistant that included a calendar, an address book, a clock, a calculator, a notepad, and email. The phone even had a touch screen with a QWERTY keyboard. But touch screens didn't make a splash until the iPhone burst onto the scene in 2007. Today the mobile phone has more computing power than old massive mainframes; touch screens are rapidly making tiny keyboards go the way of the dodo bird; and the speed of downloading and constant connection is rapidly accelerating, which means we can offer more data-rich features, like enhanced maps, on phones.

One of the most exciting parts of my job is seeking out the current boundaries of interface and sensor technology. I'm most interested in the new interactions we can offer to make devices bend and fold more and more to users' contexts to fill their needs. But, of course, we're not always going to be able to make use of the latest cool capabilities because the systems we're designing for may not support them yet, or they may not be appropriate for the site or app we're building. The budget or upper-management support to bring the system up to speed may not be there. So much of UX design has to do with the constraints of the system that your design sits on top of.

ELIMINATING THE MIDDLEMAN

I like to use the comparison of Craigslist and Airbnb to bring this home. Comparing the user experiences between related sites or apps has been a wellspring of knowledge for me in my career, offering many "aha!" moments about the kinds of user needs I should be thinking about and how newer technologies might allow for a significant enhancement in experience. One of those was the first time I used Airbnb. Both Craigslist and Airbnb allow user transactions, with Craigslist of course being a pioneer in this kind of service. The technology Craig Newmark used to build his site in 1995 and that which the designers of Airbnb took advantage of more than a decade later offer starkly contrasting experiences. If you look up the timeline for the introduction of the various versions of HTML, you'll see that the first version became available only a few years before Craigslist.org was registered. Craig Newmark was a brilliant early adopter. By contrast, Airbnb debuted in 2008, the same year as the iPhone 3G and the first public working draft of HTML5.

The enormity of how new contextual awareness through technology would change UX, like those offered by Airbnb, happened to me midsummer four years ago. A group of my close friends and I had planned a vacation to exchange the sweltering concrete jungle of New York City for a real jungle. We planned to stay at a friend's house in Puerto Rico, which was available for free, making the trip super cheap. We arrived in San Juan in the late morning and set off for our friend's house. But when we got there we saw that several windows had been broken, and when we went inside we discovered that many of the appliances were missing and the place had been trashed. Great—my friend had been robbed. There was no way we could stay there, so we suddenly needed a place for thirteen people to stay that night, within driving distance, for a nominal fee. So to my iPhone I went, expecting to have to answer a bunch of questions to narrow the search down to our needs, if we'd even be able to find options. I'd heard of Airbnb but hadn't ever used the app. When I opened it and navigated to the search box, my eye was drawn right to a blue bar above the search field, which was in fact the only bit of color on the whole page. That was good UX design pulling my eyes to the spot. Amazingly, as though the app had read my mind, it announced, "Help! I need a place, tonight!" and displayed a list of available places to rent.

Airbnb has developed an advanced website for both mobile and desktop in addition to native Android and iOS apps that make use of HTML5 Geolocation, CSS3, AJAX, and JavaScript. Its native apps also make use of SMS to reliably deliver messages to users' phones and GPS to automatically offer geolocated search results. For my search that day, just one of my phone's many sensors was used to tell the Airbnb database which of its properties to search for. The site has been programmed to "understand" that when people search on it, they're looking for a place to stay, and it starts from the assumption that the place needed is in the location the searcher is currently at.

We found a place within the hour and were on our way to what would become a great vacation. From that moment forward I was an avid Airbnb user.

Now think about Craigslist. The site has remained largely the same as when it debuted. Each layer of the Craigslist experience sits on the backbone of the original HTML, and that's by no means particularly fancy. The site hasn't been upgraded to take advantage of CSS3 to increase responsiveness, there is no AJAX to help with rapid page loading, and the JavaScript used to make the site interactive is minimal. This makes Craigslist a great case for thinking through when and how much to upgrade.

You may be thinking, "Well, Craigslist is still widely used, so upgrades don't seem to have been necessary." I'd answer, yes, so far. The site is a great example of cornering the market by being early out of the gate. Craigslist moved the dial significantly forward for individuals to interact directly with one another through the Internet; it was truly a breakthrough. Newmark was also brilliant in building from a familiar, tried-and-true model, that of newspaper classifieds. Everybody understood the model immediately, and with the huge scale the web allowed, the advantages over print versions were obvious. No UX bells and whistles were needed. But that dominant market share may be eroded before long because Craigslist has kept playing it safe. A new wave of upstarts are offering the same service but with enhanced technology.

These days the most competitive experiences come from companies that understand how to maximize the potential of products to anticipate user needs. I think of these companies as bending their systems around the needs of their customers. In order to do this well, a UX designer should know what to ask from a system and how. An enhancement you want to offer may involve significant back-end programming to make connections between required information and add in capabilities. You never want to underestimate the amount of time and money this may require or how swamped your development team is.

WORK WITHIN THE SYSTEM, BUT BE CREATIVE WITH IT

If Craigslist decided it wanted to do a big redesign, many new features could be introduced. For example, copying competitors for real estate listings, the site could add video excursions around the houses and apartments listed. But such a redesign of a popular site is a very tricky proposition that highlights a number of issues UX designers must always keep in mind.

First is that often you're simply going to have to work within the constraints of the existing system your site or app is built with. When I use the term *system* I mean back-end components (like databases, application programming interfaces, software development kits, and services that tell the computer how to interact with users, such as geolocation technology) as well as front-end capabilities that animate, allow users to navigate, and receive user input. If you're working for a large, well-established website like Craigslist, or in my case, the *Wall Street Journal*, as a UX designer you're not usually involved in determining what that system will be, and therefore the retinue of features you'll be able to include in a design is largely predetermined. But depending on the firm, you may have some input or be asked to make significant recommendations. I had virtually no say in system architecture at the *Journal*. But at Yahoo I was given more responsibility, and because the company has been going through a rebirth (a word that I don't use lightly), I've been able to ask for technologies as needed.

If you're working with a small team or are a sole operator, helping to make the choice about which system to build with may be an important part of your contribution. But if you're being asked to do a redesign, the changes the client is willing to make in the system may be quite limited due to the time and therefore money involved. You will want to give them all the newest bells and whistles, say upgrading them from a largely static old-fashioned website to a responsive one and connecting the site to whatever social network is appropriate. If you're upgrading a mobile app, maybe you'll want to take advantage of new smartphone hardware that allows them to automatically send an alert to users based on information they've been searching for. For example, you might want to alert a user who's been searching for ovens online that there is a sale on ovens at a Home Depot store she is passing by. But often you'll get pushback about such upgrades and be asked to work miracles with the system the client has.

To get over this hurdle, no matter what type of company you're working for, what kind of jobs you're working on, and what sort of team you're part of, one of the most valuable types of knowledge you can arm yourself with is a good understanding of the capabilities and constraints of the wide range of systems—iOS, Android in all its flavors, mobile web in all of its, and of course desktop web. I can't code or develop an app, but I read carefully through the documents provided to developers for each system, called "human interface guidelines," so that I can speak the language. Known as human interface guidelines across platforms, these documents are published by the manufacturers or governing bodies themselves (Apple, Google, W3C, Open Standards Initiative, etc.) to serve as specifications for each system's unique attributes. Like an architect, I may not be able to do the job of building by myself, but I understand the nature of the materials and the engineering it will take to execute my designs.

UX designers are often not programmers, but good UX is never a matter of just choosing a good selection of features and crafting an appealing and efficient design for them. You've got to learn about the options any given system gives you in order to find creative ways to work with them and push the envelope to create an enhanced user experience. All interactions are not created equal, and worse yet, all browsers aren't, either. Designers can come up with all sorts of fabulous ideas that just aren't feasible. A popular design site called Dribbble is a target of much derision for showcasing visual mocks created with no connection to the practicalities of technology and programming time. Maybe the biggest letdown designers can expose themselves to is having work shot down for this reason.

So much emphasis in most of what's written about UX design is on crafting the flow of the pages of a site or app, mapping that out with diagrams called wireframes, and designing the interface, and these flows are absolutely core to the job and great fun. I'll go into all of that in the next chapter. But in my experience, it's best if that process is done with as much knowledge of how the system you're designing for works as you can get. As soon as I started to combine an understanding of systems with my user experience perspective, I was able to explore not only more interesting ways of serving users' needs, but also ways that were reliably within the scope of possibility. I began including system information in all my designs of user flows (I'll describe the process of creating these later). This has helped me do a better job of specifying how interactions and feedback should occur. The systems you're working with define all the different ways a given task can be accomplished and how to choose the optimal one for your users.

A specific example of why this pays off is a solution I worked out for creating an ad location—a place where ads would regularly appear—on WSJ Live. One of the business requirements for the app was that we serve a static display ad somewhere. The next figure shows what the flow looked like before adding in any system information.

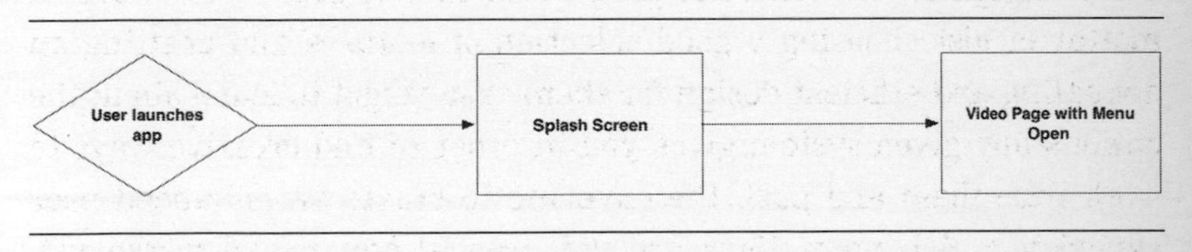

User flow of WSJ Live with no system information

Can you see a place to put an ad that won't interfere with the experience too greatly? As usual, the app would open with a splash screen, the screen that appears as an app is loading. One of the app's business requirements was that the splash screen be used for branding the app with the new WSJ Live logo. So it looks like the only place there is room for the ad is on the video-viewing home page that comes up right after that. This would be a standard option that would most likely be approved, but it doesn't go beyond the status quo, and advertisements on home pages are unappealing to users. I wanted to do better.

Now, take a look at the next figure to see what this flow tells us when we include the system details.

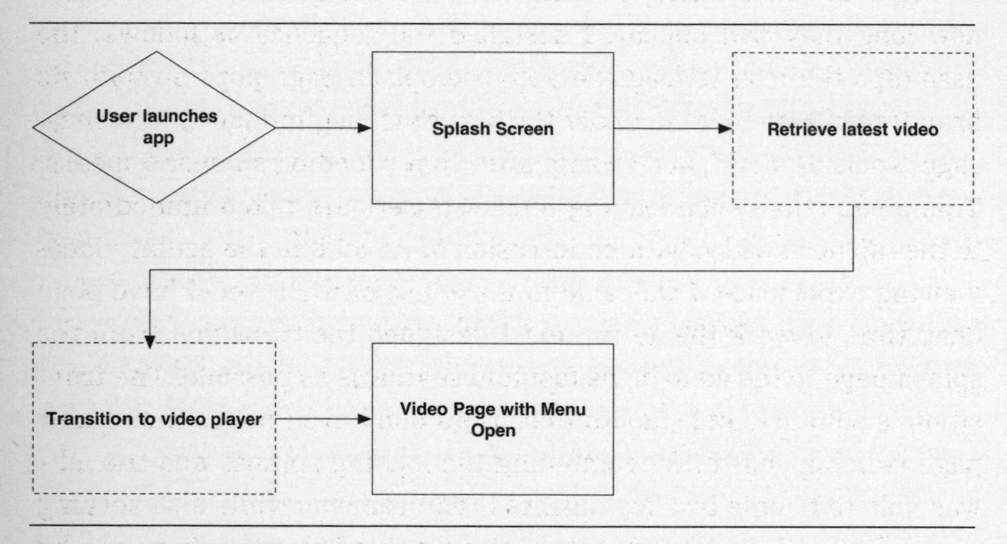

User flow of WSJ Live with system information represented with dotted lines

With this system information added, we have a clearer picture of how the loading sequence and transition to the home video-viewing page will operate. It becomes clear that time is needed to retrieve a video before the viewing page appears; a part of the design was that the app would automatically display the most recently posted video. That told me I would need a loading spinner to come up to indicate that loading was happening. Without an indication of loading activity, users are left to wonder whether an app is responding, and indicating the system status whenever a user has to wait for an action is an established usability rule. It's best if you can give an indication of how long the loading will take with a progress bar, but sometimes that's not possible because of the system. I asked the development team about this, and because different videos would load at different rates, we couldn't have a progress bar. Instead of showing just a loading spinner the whole time users were waiting, I realized that I had an opportunity to fit the ad into this process. I checked again with engineering and sure enough, the loading time would be long enough to get our ad requirement fulfilled; specifications for ads generally include for how long they will appear. I designed the sequence as follows: the user taps the icon to load the app; the splash page pops up with its branding; the ad fades in under the branding, beginning with the message "sponsored by"; and shortly after that a loading spinner appears. This means that when loading finishes, users are taken immediately to the top news video with no intrusion of an ad into the actual video-viewing experience. I was able to make use of what would have been dead time to work the ad in, and I designed the transition from the splash page to the ad to be as fast and seamless as possible. The transition is so quick and smooth that users don't even notice that a new page is being shown. By combining the loading spinner and the ad I was able to handle two key business requirements while also serving a usability goal. I've found that the timing of system operations can be very helpful in finding places to consolidate interactions and include product requirements.

THE NEW SYSTEMS SMORGASBORD

These days there is a huge number of system capabilities for any given device that you should consider when crafting designs. The iPhone 5S, for example, has a chip dedicated to location services, which takes a load off the other chips when processing this data. The iPhone 5C does not. A UX designer with this knowledge can trust in the location chip to keep a 5S user's battery from draining and go ahead and include features that draw on location services without fear the app will be unpopular because it eats up too much power. All the iPhones have infrared proximity sensors, which allow for designing interactions that don't require the user to actually touch the screen. One example is theremin apps, which allow you to make music by waving your hand over the phone. They're a twenty-first century version of an actual instrument created by Russian inventor Léon Theremin in 1920 that made eerie-sounding music when the player waved his hands over two electronic antennas. The iPhone also includes a magnetometer that powers a compass in the phone, which means that apps can tell users not only what their location is with GPS, but also what direction they're heading in, which can make figuring out if you're going the right way easier. Most smartphones include a light sensor, which can be used, for example, to make adjustments to the brightness of the display based on the level of ambient light in a room. That's a lovely feature to build into an app. All smartphones have audio inputs and outputs to facilitate interactions like speech dictation or the services that power the Shazam music app, which records the music playing wherever you are, sends it to a server, identifies it, and sends the info back to the user with links for online stores to make purchases right then. When you combine all the information you can about capabilities like these to create apps, the results can be truly amazing. If you don't know what each of these system features does and how it can be worked into a site or app, you won't be pushing the limits of the UX you might be able to create.

It's important to learn the differences between the front-end (client side) systems and back-end ones that run on the server in order to understand which interactions can be accomplished by the device a user is on and which will require database calls—such as searching a large data set. This will help you when designing feedback for loading something that might take more time than you'd want, such as pulling up photos from the web or from a local database. Or maybe you want to include autofill of user information on your page; you've got to know whether the system can support this and how quickly the information can be retrieved.

It's also important to understand the distinction between programming for the web and the object-oriented programming that is done for mobile systems like iOS and Android. They're very different and each has its own capabilities and limits that you'll need to be aware of. Until recently, the programming with which websites are built didn't allow for resizing to fit mobile screens, so if you wanted to be on mobile, you'd have to go with object-oriented programming and an app. But then responsive design was developed, and suddenly you could design websites with responsive capabilities baked in and you had to start thinking about how to optimize one design across desktop and mobile platforms.

Perhaps you've had good training in the inner workings of a wide range of systems. If you've taken high school computer classes, human-computer interaction (HCI) classes, or classes in information and library science and digital design, you probably do. But many people come to UX design without that kind of education. One thing you can do is take some classes, which is definitely advised. Learning the front-end languages (meaning getting up to speed with HTML5, CSS3, and JavaScript) may not be required to work in UX, but knowledge of them will be of great help in crafting your designs and getting good reception from your development team. And as I'll discuss later, the new hybrid UX developers, who have both sets of skills, are becoming more and more sought after.

I've also found some self-teaching methods very helpful. For one, I read through the various human interface guidelines previously mentioned, which are written to provide a good set of rules for developers to follow for visual design and the treatment of interactions. They fill you in on the full range of capabilities, such as the gestures that can be included, like touch, swipe and drag, and double touch; the tools for navigation, like the back button versus the up button in Android; and the types of notification messages that are supported. Many cross-platform guidelines are now available, and these really help in figuring out how to optimize for desktop versus mobile.

You may not agree with everything the guidelines suggest. For example, the Android design guidelines include the tip that "Real objects are more fun than buttons and menus. Allow people to directly touch and manipulate objects in your app. It reduces the cognitive effort needed to perform a task while making it more emotionally satisfying."[1] You might be more of a minimalist and think that such representations of real-world objects, such as the envelope icon for Gmail or the calendar page icon for Google Calendar, are old-fashioned and overly obtrusive. The interface guidelines for Android suggest the use of an action bar for apps that highlights the most common actions performed for a given page, and you may not be a fan of that device. But the guidelines are a treasure trove of information about how you might design your product and any limits or new features you must be aware of.

In addition, the standards issued by the World Wide Web Consortium (W3C) serve as the almanac for web technologies, describing all of them and offering best practices. You can go there to read about JavaScript, for example, or what scripting interfaces are available, or what all the types of graphical interfaces are.

Once you've learned these basics, you can learn a great deal more by asking good questions of your developer. Luckily, I'm usually met with friendliness when I go bother my developers with questions like "How do we show a spinner and an ad on the splash page without adding another screen to the flow?" If you aren't technically proficient, I'd suggest making friends with someone who is. Your career could depend on it. I'm not a programmer, and mine definitely did.

Another way I've learned a great deal about system capabilities and the creative things that can be programmed is by just using as many apps and sites as I can. As I write this I have 397 apps on my iPhone 5, the majority of which are there only for reference when I want to see how a particular issue is being addressed, such as search and filter tasks, commerce experiences, and content strategy. One process

I found hugely beneficial when I first got into UX was taking screenshots from the different apps I used. I then imported these images into my drawing program, OmniGraffle, and traced each interface element down to the details, like the tracing I made of a page of the Spotify app, shown in the next figure.

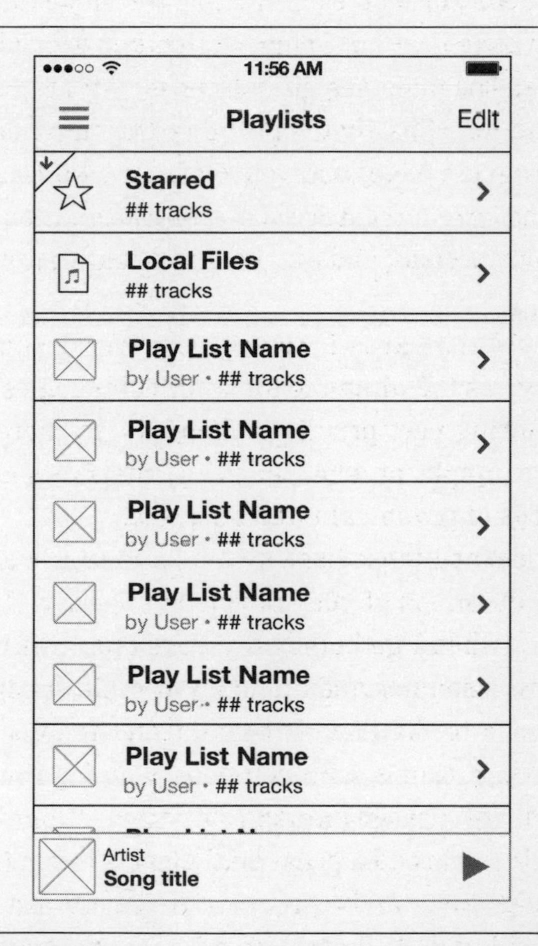

A tracing of the Spotify app. Objects with a different color indicate their presence as optional.

By performing this exercise over and over I learned about many of the interface components that are similar across apps, such as menus, toolbars, and headers, and how they differ between systems. I learned that variations generally exist because of updates to operating systems and software that have been made in response to usability studies and other UX analysis to identify improvements. As I became familiar with each product's design, I could start to see the logic behind the interface and I found I could reverse engineer tasks from those designs when creating my own.

In addition to becoming fluent in standard elements of Apple and Android apps, I took special note of custom elements and began to appreciate why the designers of the apps that used them decided to stray from the norm.

This experience was hugely helpful to me when I began to create my own wireframes and craft original interfaces, so much so that I've made it a part of all the classes I teach. The goal is to get to the state where you're able to begin designing from this rich base of precedents rather than trying to start from scratch each time.

This leads to an important point about systems constraints: many of them can be your best friends in crafting a design.

YOU DON'T NEED TO REINVENT THE WHEEL

So many designers—including me—would love to focus on custom designs, but sometimes you just can't customize, whether because of the time and money resources committed to the project or a system constraint. I got a great lesson in this when I was working on a custom feature for the Yahoo Finance app.

We had prototyped a set of tips that popped up at specific moments, such as when a user landed on certain pages for the first time. The idea was to help users learn about the app over time, as needed, rather than giving a boring tutorial all at once. I had designed the tips using animation and a strong contrasting visual treatment to try to focus the user's attention on them. Much to my dismay, five out of nine people tested did not read the tips, either because they didn't notice them or because they didn't care for pop-ups. So much for my customization.

Meanwhile, I saw that a feature of the same app prototype, which was a requirement of the iOS system, was being used by all nine of the subjects tested. This was a standard UIAlertView notification, which must be used in iOS to ask for permission to send push notifications to users—the rectangular pop-up you see all the time in iOS that typically has "OK" and "Cancel" buttons on it. They are required in order to centralize settings for all the apps and to provide security. Just about everything in the pop-up alert is standardized, from the way it animates to the color, size, shape, and number of options it can present. The only things you can customize are the text and the button labels. Absolutely every iOS app must adhere to this.

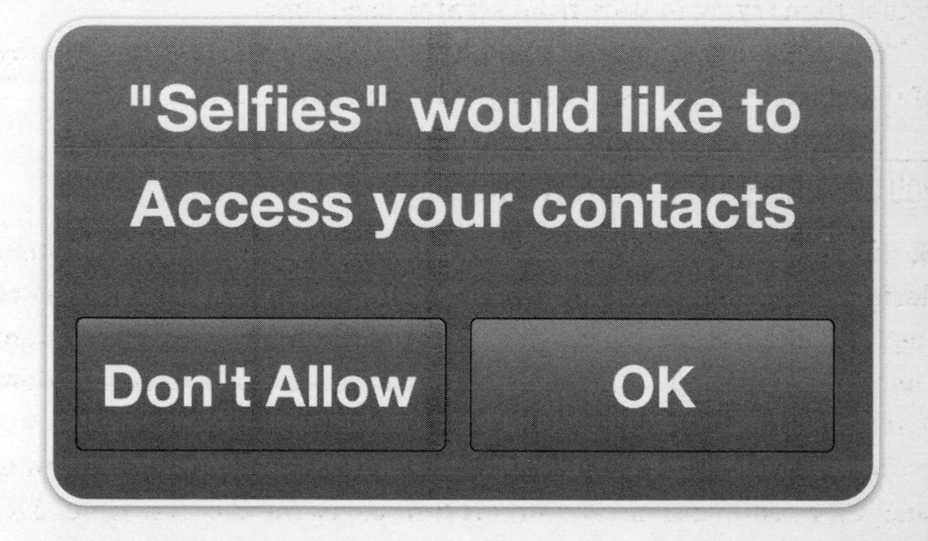

An iOS UIAlertView from iOS1-6. The same colors, animation, placement, and number of buttons appear on nearly all UIAlertViews.

What struck me was how effective the UIAlertView was because it was so familiar. All of those tested actually read this alert message, tapped "OK" or "Cancel," and moved on. They didn't gripe about it as a pop-up and they did exactly what was needed. I think this pop-up has grown so familiar to users because of its ubiquity that the response has actually become Pavlovian. That is exactly how I want my Yahoo users to behave when interacting with a pop-up, because it means no interference with engagement to the app has occurred. This is just one case of how a system constraint can be beneficial, helping to make interactions familiar and accepted.

Windows Phone and Android have similar standardized elements, and the web has its own set of standards. A number of highly detailed frameworks for interface design are also available now, such as Bootstrap, developed by Twitter, and include predesigned navigation, alerts, icons, loading indicators, and styles for content. They give you just about everything you will need to get a project up and running without having to worry about untested interface elements. They can be customized a bit, but the idea is that their out-of-the-box state is a tried-and-true model for a usable experience.

I see custom interfaces hailed all the time as great experiences by design blogs and the Apple App Store because of how well tailored they are to the particular experience they solve. No question, many of them introduce great innovations, but before you attempt these yourself I highly recommend that you address why you would move from the standard to begin with. A clear rationalization can help you get along a whole lot better with your developers. Once you understand enough about the systems they must work in, you appreciate the level of effort involved in bringing a custom interface to life. Creating one can cause all kinds of headaches—perhaps better described as migraines—and if it's not polished, that can be your worst nightmare because of the size of its impact on the feel of a product. Rebuilding things like custom transition animations or touch events painstakingly polished by other developers can be a huge task. It's important to thoughtfully evaluate how much benefit a custom interface might provide users against the costs in time, money, and developer frustration—as well as your own—involved in making it. Of course, your developers can apprise you of the hassle involved, and trust me, they won't hold back. But it's much preferable that you be thinking in these terms as you're formulating your plans for the product.

Don't get me wrong, I think custom interfaces are cool. My favorite apps have a look and feel all their own, and I aspire to make experiences that fit in that category. They can also be used on multiple platforms because they don't adhere to a particular platform's patterns and thus don't feel out of place on one device versus another. There's definitely a place in the world for them, but you should always keep in mind that for people who don't see apps through a designer's eyes, your and your team's effort may just not be appreciated and therefore may not be worthwhile.

Keeping up with the interfaces a system allows for and offers is particularly important because so much of UX design concerns figuring out which interfaces to include. I've spent a good deal of time exploring the intricacies of user interface elements, and that familiarity has allowed me to gauge much better how to accomplish a given task, such as using a picker menu, which organizes options vertically, making them easier to scan, rather than a slider, which displays them horizontally. The pace of innovation is incredible, and as I said before, this is one of the things I love about the job. A year ago I wouldn't have been able to write that I understand how sensors like an accelerometer are used in conjunction with an animation that is coded in Core Animation versus OpenGL. (Translation: Open GL is a web standard, and if you use it for a mobile phone, you may see slower action in adjusting to users holding the phone one way or the other than if you use Core Animation, which is iOS specific.)

KNOW YOUR DATA AND HOW IT CAN BE USED

In graduate school I had to take a class called Databases. I dreaded it and I put it off until my last year. Ironically, the class was one of the most valuable I took during my time at the UNC Chapel Hill School of Information and Library Science. Learning about the relationships that data can have with other data opened up the world of UX to me. I began to imagine how a product could work better based on the kind of data available, seeing the potential connections that could be made between types of information.

To those of you unfamiliar with databases I highly recommend picking up an introductory book or other resource on the web. There are many that are free. You can even start messing around with MySQL, the open source database management language, for free on the MySQL site, which also offers free webinars. All you want here is a high-level theoretical understanding. Database design is the central nervous system of all web products, and understanding the basics of database structures and capabilities is the starting point for what you'll be able to do on the front end.

What I walked away with from my class wasn't going to get me a job managing databases or even enough confidence to say I knew SQL, but I did get a more informed understanding of how much the structure of data in a system I'm working with has to do with determining the kinds of features I can, and want to, design into a product. If you want navigation based on tags that organize similar items together in a product, that comes from the database. If you want to let users enter an instruction to have your app send them a notification, such as "Remind me to buy milk today," you'll need a database that can interpret natural language. You'll also better understand how to design features that mitigate how long calls to the database take and the kinds of errors to watch out for. Learning more about the back end doesn't just help you design better ways to perform tasks, like navigating or inputting data; it also helps you create experiences that avoid common pitfalls, like badly constructed responses to search queries.

If we don't understand the nature of the data the site or app has to work with and the nature of how it can be accessed, we risk wasting time trying to design a function or feature that just isn't supported. During my time at the *Wall Street Journal*, much to my lament, the articles on the website did not know what section they belonged in. This was due to no fault of the developers. The higher-ups hadn't budgeted for time to correct the problem. The result was a painful design review in which a product idea that had been approved by my boss was shot down by the engineering team because they simply couldn't make it happen. All of this learning about systems may sound like a real chore, but trust me, it will prevent such frustrations, and you will start seeing the payoffs immediately. When you're up to speed on the wide range of capabilities of the various systems, you can really start to have fun with innovating. It's like playing with Legos, discovering the remarkable creations that can come out of new ways of connecting the fundamental system components.

AUGMENTED REALITY FOR FINGERNAILS

Never did my knowledge of tech allow me to think out of the box more than on the day I heard a great idea for an app that sent my mind spinning with ways to design its system. All the ideas that popped into my head sprang from knowledge of available technical solutions. It happened during a take-your-kid-to-work day at Dow Jones, when I was asked to help run an activity with the kids for an hour because I work with mobile technology and the kids love their mobile devices so much.

We gave them all crayons and printouts of an empty iPad and had them draw ideas for apps. The only instruction was to imagine ways to control their apps using as many fingers or as few as possible. As an app creator I was really intrigued to see what they could do with their imaginations. They came up with loads of great ideas, from games with worlds as rich as those created by the blockbuster AAA video game studios to homework helpers powered by artificial intelligence capable of slicing through time spent on the most confounding math problems. Near the end of the hour an eight-year-old girl came up to present. I projected her drawing to the class and saw an outline of a hand with all five fingers stretched out, each one ending with a fingernail painted in vibrant colors. The boys in the class immediately burst out heckling. One yelled a long and loud "Ewwww!" I responded, "That's half of all the people in the world you are saying 'ew' to. If you want to make something great, you should appeal to everyone!" Might as well get them started with UX early!

This point seemed to go over well, because the boys got quiet really fast. The eight-year-old went on to explain how the app would let people take a photograph of the backs of their hands and then paint their fingernails in the image. The class applauded and the little girl went back to her seat. After the session was over and the kids were gone, my mind was ablaze with all the great ideas they had come up with. Most of them were so imaginative that the work necessary to make them a reality would be Herculean, not to mention requiring the Midas touch. AAA video game studios and pioneers of artificial intelligence don't come cheap. But the fingernail idea stuck in my head. Would it work with augmented reality technology, I wondered, to project the images onto your hands after you've finished? Could you zoom in to get a fine level of detail as you decorated the nails? Was there a library of patterns or multiple kinds of brushes you could cycle through to make really detailed nail art? Could you save and share your creations? When you finished, might it be possible to print the nail designs out as stickers for purchase? Maybe they could actually then be applied to a person's real nails. When would it be available?!

The idea swelled with potential once the systems capabilities were factored in.

NATIVE OR WEB?

One of the biggest systems issues all web developers and designers must grapple with today is whether to use web technology or native design technology—do we want to build a website or an app? The system rules that we have to follow when designing apps are different from those for websites.

My students often ask me which they should use, web or native? My answer depends on what kind of experience they want the system to support. If the users' needs are informational, such as location, hours of operation, and the menu for a restaurant, or if the client is publishing a stream of articles all in the same format and wants to reach the largest possible audience, I would probably say they should go with web. With responsive design, websites can be viewed well on mobile devices, and designing for the web makes you accessible to a wider user base. The web can be called on by any device with a browser, but apps can only be used by the owners of the devices that support that type of app, i.e., iOS apps don't work on Android. You can, of course, design apps for all, or most, devices, but that's extra time and money.

If, on the other hand, interactivity is key—say you're designing a game, social network, or activity tracker—then I'd probably say an app is the better way to go, because the web doesn't handle interactivity as well as apps do. It would require supplemental frameworks to do so.

Trade-offs

Both web and native technologies have minuses as well as pluses, and you've got to weigh them carefully. Once, in one of my classes, a student was presenting his project. He had designed what he described as an app, with a mobile Safari interface design, which meant that it was in fact a web application. He had made this choice so that users wouldn't have to go through an app store to download it; they could go through mobile Safari or some other browser and then navigate to the proper URL. But in his presentation, when he got to the design for one page, he said, "Then users tap here to take a photo of themselves."

To which I responded, "You can't do that on the web."

"That's okay, this is an app," he said.

"Then why are people accessing it through a browser?" I asked.

The student turned to his design, then back to me, then back to his design again, and promptly crossed out the button for taking photos, saying, "Okay, no more problem!"

"Wasn't that an important part of the experience?" I asked.

He smartly responded, "Not as important as accessing it anywhere."

You've got to seriously consider which is your priority, interactivity or a larger audience.

THE ADVANTAGES OF WEB VERSUS APP

I was working at the *Wall Street Journal* when responsive web design made its way onto the scene. The *Boston Globe* revealed a redesign of its site, and as we widened and narrowed our browser windows everyone got a little jealous. The *Globe* had one design that worked on iPhone, iPad, and all the different Android phones and tablets. Granted, you couldn't find the site in an app store, but there was something amazing about how elegant their solution was. Our head of design technology had reviewed the new system, and he wanted to explore how we might employ it to give our users a better experience than our current mobile site. I and the other UX designer on the team dove into the new framework, and I learned a great deal about the grid our desktop website sat on. The grid is a relatively easy concept: a web page is *x* (say 1,000 pixels) wide; divide that by *y* (10) and you get the units (ten 100-pixel units). Then you measure each module on the web page, such as Most Popular Stories or the navigation bar for the number of units it takes up. (For a deeper understanding of designing for a grid, check out Khoi Vinh's book *Ordering Disorder: Grid Principles for Web Design*.) The thing that is so great about responsive design is that it allows modules to look and behave differently when displayed in different widths so that they can be optimized for each size. The most useful takeaway for me, though, was not about optimizing the look and feel of displays. The most useful takeaway was that with responsive you don't have to design a bunch of modules, some for desktop only because they need hover states or mobile only because they need gestures. When you have only a few fundamental modules that are malleable, you have less visual design work to do, which in turn means less chance of inconsistencies. Most of all it means less development time to create and maintain your products.

That doesn't mean switching to a responsive design is easy, though. When I left the *Journal* the team was still in the process of building the new responsive site, and they still are.

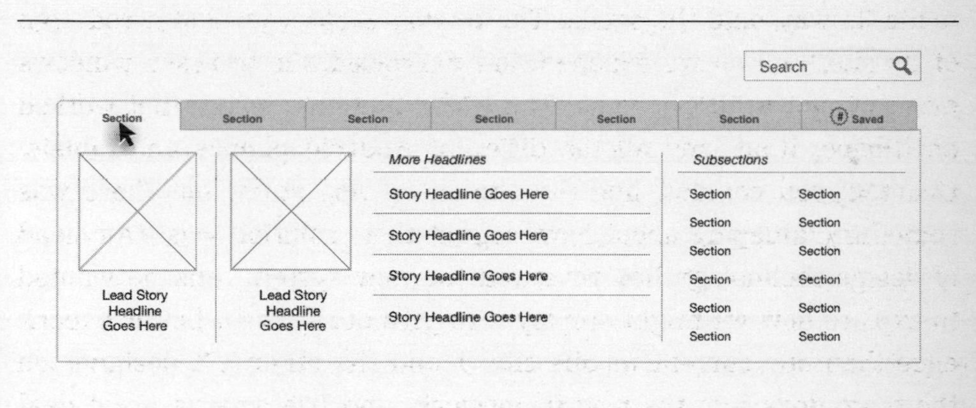

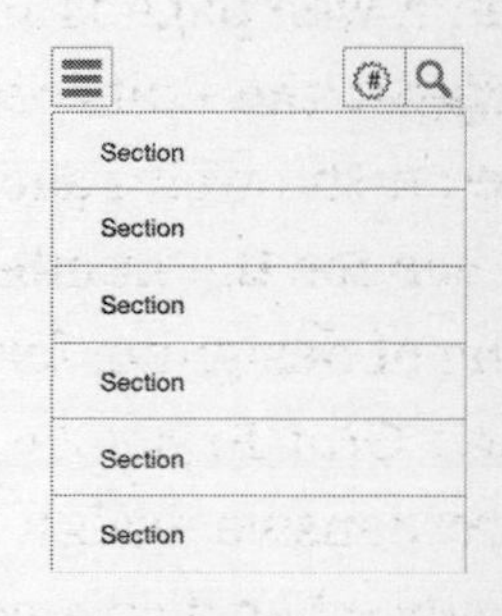

Top: Desktop navigation module with hover state drop downs. Bottom left: Tablet navigation module. No longer supports hover states. Bottom right: Mobile navigation module. No longer supports hover states. Section drop down extends to needed length.

DON'T BECOME OVERLY HABITUATED

When I have to design for a system that I don't normally use, work gets hard. All of us, designers and users, become habituated to the systems we use most. My own habits as an iOS user are different from those of an Android or Windows Phone user. I still have a hard time using the back button on Android devices when I switch over from using my iPhone. Understanding the little details of each platform will help you be aware of polishes that users will really get pissed off about if you forget or ignore them. I once showed the drawing below to a class of mostly iPhone users and asked the Android owners to tell me what it was.

They had no idea because it was using the language of another system. If you want to become a good UX designer, you have to become multi-system-lingual.

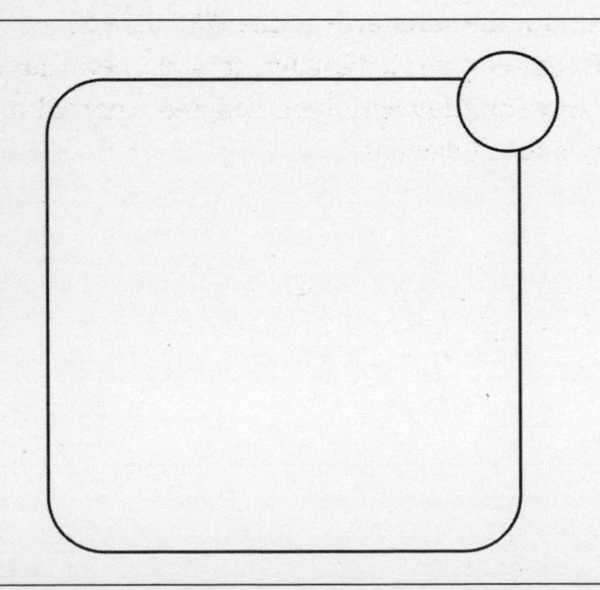

An iOS app icon with a badge in the top right is unfamiliar to Android users.

POINTS TO REMEMBER

Creativity Loves Constraints

» Don't think of the constraints of the systems or the requirements you have to work with as limitations; think of them as a foundation for building a creative design.

» Even though technology evolves rapidly, its adoption is always incremental. Always seek out the current boundaries of technology, but don't get too far ahead of user and business goals in introducing it.

» Take the time to learn as much as you can about the capabilities and limits of the systems you're designing for. This will greatly enhance your ability to craft optimal user flows and work in new features and interactions.

» It's important to understand the differences between the front- and back-end systems, as well as those between operating systems. Read the interface guidelines provided and become familiar with the standards of the W3C as well.

» Don't become overly habituated to one operating system; be sure to stay familiar with both iOS and Android and with the broader range of devices.

Chapter 3

INTERFACE DESIGNS ARE THE FACIAL EXPRESSIONS OF DIGITAL PRODUCTS

In his brilliantly titled book *Turn Signals Are the Facial Expressions of Automobiles*, published in 1993, Donald Norman lamented how unattuned the design of so many products is to human desires and needs, illuminating how good design can give any object, from refrigerators to the directional signals of cars, personality, sensitivity, and engagement. Everyone understood the emotional appeal of a well-designed automobile (my favorite being the 1983 Porsche 911), but how many had thought about all the little interactions we have with cars as a form of conversation? Product design has come a long way in the decades since Norman made his case, and meanwhile computer technology has ushered in an era of machines that truly do converse with us, some more enjoyably than others.

Those German drivers mentioned in chapter 1 aren't the only ones for whom electronic voices have raised hackles. Who hasn't been annoyed now and then at that overly insistent TomTom or Garmin telling us to "Turn left at the fork. Turn LEFT at the fork." And when the machine says it's "recalibrating," it's almost as though we hear it mumbling to itself, "You feebleminded human, I *told* you to turn left."

But our ability to make machines speak to us and interact with us in more natural and pleasing ways is evolving at a remarkable rate. Some machines now even have body language. The personal assistant robots mentioned in chapter 1 evoked a wide range of emotional responses, and a whole new breed of robots is being crafted that will be much more evocative. The design of some humanoid robots has already become so sophisticated that they really can make us feel that they're actually alive. Scientists at MIT have developed a group of small, humanlike robots with the foot size of a three-year-old, whose "facial" expressions are extraordinarily rich with emotion, as shown in the next figure.

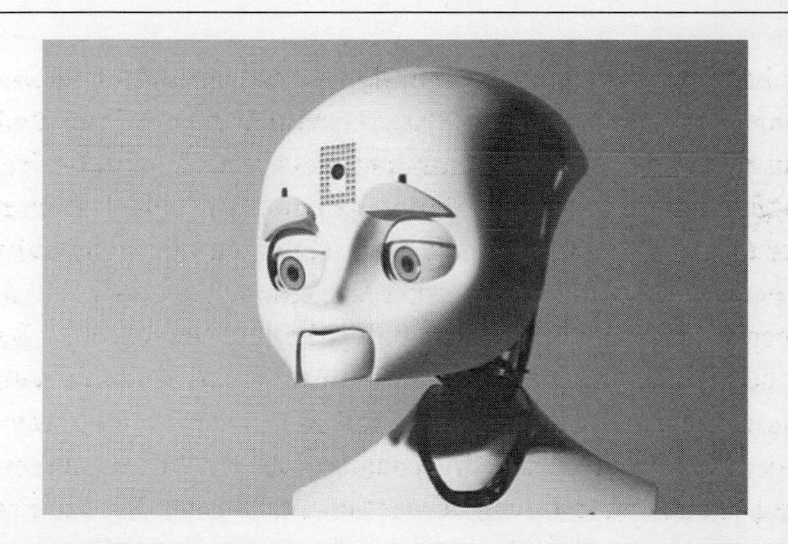

(Courtesy of Humanoid Robotics Group)

Software designers, too, have been rapidly developing an incredible repertoire of tools for bringing digital products to life and making them entertaining and emotionally evocative. Software has come a long way from its origins.

It used to be that software was purely utilitarian. The name *computer* even speaks to the computational nature of the functions originally performed. Today, though, many features developed in software have been created specifically to delight us—think of the addictive appeal of the iPhone's audio notifications of a new email or text, or the swooshing sound Samsung tablets make when you swipe to unlock the screen. One of my favorites is the sound the fashion retail app Gilt makes at noon every day to alert you that a sale has begun. My response is Pavlovian, right down to the salivating.

Software has been making our interactions with our desktops and mobile devices so much more engaging and full of life that, like those robotic three-year-olds, our computers have begun to seem almost sentient—capable of perceiving and of feeling.

In the credits for the 1968 film *2001: A Space Odyssey*, the computer HAL 9000 is listed as a character. HAL stands for Heuristically programmed ALgorithmic computer, and "he" is not only conscious, he even has his own emotions. So much so that he has what the film's director, Stanley Kubrick, described as an emotional breakdown. He's overwhelmed by his distress at being told by mission command to withhold from the crew information about where the ship is going and what the mission is. After HAL goes on a (spoiler alert) killing spree that earns him position number 13 on the American Film Institute's list of the hundred greatest film villains, the last crew member alive, mission pilot Dave, begins shutting HAL down. In one of the most eerie and haunting sequences in the history of film, the machine calls out plaintively, "I'm afraid. I'm afraid, Dave. Dave, my mind is going. I can feel it." The viewer actually feels sympathy for him. I should say "it," but it's impossible not to think of HAL as a he.

Thirteen years after the date that the fictional HAL nearly killed his entire crew, computers are embedded in our lives as much if not more than Arthur C. Clarke and Stanley Kubrick envisioned. And the Internet of Things has just gotten started. We haven't quite learned how to make our computers actually think and feel yet, but we have learned a whole lot about how to make them make *us* feel.

In this chapter I want to show you the value of thinking of your work the way those who created HAL thought of bringing him to life (though, unless you're designing a game that's meant to be spooky, not for the purposes of scaring the bejeezus out of people). The key is thinking of yourself as a storyteller and designing with all the complexity and richness of human emotion in mind. My earliest attempts at creating sites were too mechanical. I focused purely on hitting the baseline for what my competitors were making or what interface guidelines stated were the best practices. My designs weren't coming from the heart. That may sound silly, but if emotion is a part of what we intend to offer users, then some input needs to come from inside us rather than a manual.

WHAT MAKES A GOOD STORY?

It was the best of times, it was the worst of times...
Charles Dickens, *A Tale of Two Cities*

Call me Ishmael.
Herman Melville, *Moby Dick*

As Gregor Samsa awoke one morning from uneasy dreams he found himself transformed in his bed into a gigantic insect.
Franz Kafka, *The Metamorphosis*

These are the opening lines of three of the greatest stories ever told. I'd venture that those of us who have read these books will always be able to name the book the line is from in a flash, even many decades after reading them. Even lots of people who haven't read these books can tell you where these lines are from. They've been so influential that they've made their way into the collective cultural consciousness.

As UX designers, maybe we can't hope to tell a story as well as Dickens, Melville, or Kafka, but we *are* storytellers, and this is one of the most enjoyable aspects of the job. The kinds of stories we tell are different in many ways from novels, films, songs, and symphonies, which are all forms of storytelling of their own. But there are some fundamental similarities as well.

Every story has a beginning, a middle, and an end. Which doesn't at all mean that a story has to unfold in that order. Take the case of the story usually attributed to Ernest Hemingway that is all of six words long:

For sale: baby shoes, never worn.

I still get goose bumps every time I read that. The story proceeds from the end, to the beginning, to the middle. A baby has been born (baby shoes), but some tragedy has happened (never worn), so the shoes are for sale (the end). What an emotional wallop from six little words. The story also pulls us in; it has an interactivity to it. Hemingway makes us figure out the drama, creating a sense of mystery for that fleeting moment we're left to wonder why the shoes have never been worn. And, of course, it's marvelously efficient. There are many wonderful stories that are very long—anyone read Proust?—but that doesn't mean their authors wasted words. Truly good storytellers always move their stories along at a good pace, and any given passage, even if it seems to be a long digression, will have clear relevance to the larger story eventually.

But the art of storytelling is also always evolving, and it too has come a long way since its inception. Experts in human evolution think that the first stories were told for utilitarian purposes of survival. They developed to literally save our lives by giving warnings of dangerous places, people, or animals. Now, of course, many stories are told purely for entertainment purposes, but stories are still a potent method—

probably the most potent—for teaching information, for persuasion, and for engagement. UX designers most fundamentally want the work we do to be effective, meaning we want to help our users make decisions with the tools or utilities we produce. As with any tool or utility, our designs must focus on serving a need. But who says the service of that need can't be lively, entertaining, and even emotionally evocative? In this chapter, I'll discuss the ways in which you can make sure it is.

ISN'T THE STORY SOMEONE ELSE'S JOB?

You might think that the story of your product is told primarily by its branded elements, such as the company logo; other branded graphical elements, such as color schemes; and its content—that's for the marketing team, content strategists, and visual designers to work out. For sure, brand imperatives and the content the company provides are key elements of the storytelling your product does—they set the tone. The branding design elements are the first layer of tone. But your interface design is also vital to any product's story. When you design a dynamic, moving, smart interface, you play the role of narrator. You will also generally be responsible for the actual narration about how to navigate the site, writing the copy used for labels and input boxes, such as "Enter billing information" and "Click here to move to shopping cart," to use two pedestrian examples. As I'll cover later, the skill with which you write these directives and explanations can have a great deal to do with how effective the story you tell is.

In terms of the brand story, it's for sure that you are always going to be designing for a brand, whether it's a big corporate product group or a not-for-profit, a government organization, or a university. They will all have a brand story that your product must be telling, and this will both constrain and guide you, as I described regarding my work on the *Wall Street Journal* apps. At the *Journal* my work always had to be sensitive to the company's old and well-established brand identity. The phrase "business news and designs" still rings in my ears, but the truth is that having a strong brand story was really helpful.

You never want to violate or interfere with brand messaging in any way in your designs—and they're not likely to be approved if you do. For some products, you need to be very careful that your interfaces don't overpower the content. With a brand like the *Journal*, the content is king; anything too flashy that distracts from that is just not going to fly. For other products, like a new app, your interface may be a big part of the content. For example, Sleep Cycle is an alarm clock app that analyzes people's sleep patterns. The app was designed with some thoughtful UX that tells its story—which is that it wants to help you get good sleep—with nice touches, such as the screen going dark when it comes time for you to go to sleep at night. In the daytime the app is filled with informational and utilitarian interfaces, such as the familiar scrollable clock dial for setting alarms (also used in the stock Clock app from Apple), and a graphic portraying when you were in deep sleep or more restless sleep during the prior night. You always have to make your interfaces consistent with the brand message and personality, but that doesn't mean you can't be really creative within those bounds. And sometimes you'll have a good deal of latitude.

With work for startups, which are just building their brand identity, you usually get the opportunity to help substantially mold and shape that identity with your product. You're still given detailed requirements and marketing material to guide the design, but you have more influence to suggest innovations. You might also be involved in helping to rebrand a company, as I've been at Yahoo. The overarching directive for my team at Yahoo is to make each app use images in an interesting way to give the products a more luxurious feel. If you look at Yahoo Weather, which won an Apple Design Award for 2013, you'll find a wonderful selection of photos of your location depicting the appropriate weather conditions, which we've crowdsourced from Flickr users, displayed behind the weather information. For Yahoo Finance, we had to tweak this concept. Most of the photos associated with the content that came up at first were of old white guys in suits. We needed to tell a different story. A thought hit me. Living in New York, I was well aware of the iconic bull of Wall Street, but it would be boring to look at that same image over and over. I had to start thinking more deeply about the content and the users. The app was covering the global markets. So I started looking through Flickr for images of other world markets. Sure enough, the architecture and landmarks around the NASDAQ, Hang Seng, FTSE, and Nikkei markets made for great imagery. We ended up using photos from the different exchanges as backgrounds to the financial data and changing them according to the timing of the opening of each market.

Screenshot of the Yahoo Finance iOS app

Even if the brand elements are firmly established, there is so much you can do. Netflix has been brilliantly creative in designing its interactions aimed at kids, making use of animations with favorite characters from cartoons and books. In the iPad app, for example, there is a button on the home page labeled "Just for Kids," and when users first click on the button an animation tutorial starts that features characters from Disney and Nickelodeon. When I clicked on the button one time, it literally unhinged and the character Stitch from Disney's *Lilo & Stitch* jumped out from underneath the button, as if it were a hatch leading to a hidden world. Stitch then waved at me, inviting me to follow him, and jumped back into the button. What a great story. What kid wouldn't want to jump through a hatchway with a beloved character into a world of cartoons?

The first step in going beyond the basic story of the brand requirements is to think through the implications of the larger category of the site or app you're working on.

WHAT GENRE IS YOUR STORY?

"It was a dark and stormy night" is clearly the opening of a mystery (Edward Bulwer-Lytton's 1830 novel *Paul Clifford*), and "When I look back on my childhood, I wonder how I survived at all" is obviously the start of either an autobiographical novel or a memoir (Frank McCourt's *Angela's Ashes*). Just as in fiction and film, with sites and apps, you have established genres to play with that can start you off in thinking about the type of story you want to tell. That doesn't mean you have to slavishly follow preordained rules—you always want to be applying creativity, for sure. But just as with learning about your users and about the constraints of the system, constantly keeping in mind the genre of the product is a huge help in crafting designs. It's another creativity-boosting constraint.

Are you creating an e-commerce site? Are you building a community platform? Is your site delivering news, and if so, is that hard news or entertainment news? The answers to these questions should lead you in very different directions. One case I love to use in my classes is the contrast between two sites that offer wedding planning services. One of them, TheKnot.com, features a barrage of boxes on the home page with photos of dresses, cakes, rings, and venues, as well as several ads. It looks just like an e-commerce site, which may be fine if people are coming to the site primarily to shop.

The other site, WeddingLovely.com, is focused on building a relationship with the user by helping her to plan, so the home page of the site tells a very different story, and it does so masterfully, packing a powerful emotional punch. The page features one large, full-bleed photo of a couple in their wedding attire holding hands and standing before a gorgeous ocean landscape—it puts the user right in the middle of the action and sets a warm emotional tone. There are no ads, and the text that's run over the image says loud and clear what the site is for—"Guided online wedding planning"—above a brightly colored box that draws the eye to it and says, "Start planning your wedding." This site is elegantly conveying that it's going to take the user on an exciting, emotionally satisfying journey; it's going to make the planning process not only nice and simple, but an adventure. It's also clearly conveying that it's all about helping the user, not just marketing to her.

GUIDING YOUR EVERY STEP

It seems the best lessons are always learned right after you could have used them most. I learned about the mandate for storytelling during a review of my team's design for the Yahoo Finance app in which my boss told us how ill prepared the product was. "What's the story?" he asked. "How does this fit in with the story of your user; how does it fit the problem that you're trying to solve?" I had no good answers. From then on, I've taken those questions to heart, and I make sure to apply them to every screen, every message, every interaction I'm designing.

A couple weeks after that embarrassing meeting, when we were again presenting the design, we presented a larger story about the app. We described a day in the life of the user and how the app would be an integral part of that day, showing how it would present to her the most relevant financial news and data from around the world as the day unfolded. The concept of using photos from each of the world markets and timing them to the market openings fit right in with this story. Not only did this work in the presentation—our boss approved the concept—but it also worked for me every step of the way as I was drawing the interfaces and thinking through how users would enter the site and the journeys they would go on through it. I found this helped me think about the emotions users would be having and also what their expectations would be about what the app would let them do and how it would respond to their changing needs.

Whatever their motivations to use your product, users will come to it with hopes and expectations, and those are colored by some feeling or range of feelings. Maybe your user is driving to work and is worried he'll be late for a meeting. Say your app is Waze, the community-based traffic navigation app. Take a look at the story Waze might be telling him in the next figure.

The Waze design could be purely informational; the map could be just a traditional lines-and-road-names format. But Waze has some fun with it, creating a little cartoon world. The information is front and center and extremely clear—that's the overriding imperative—but the story is, "We know it's no fun to commute, so we're going to make it at least a little fun for you, and we're going to tell you everything you need to know to get you there on time." No wonder Google bought Waze for $1.1 billion.

The emotions your users show up with and the hopes and desires they'll bring with them vary wildly. Say you're working on a *Star Wars*-related app. I can say from personal experience you'll have high

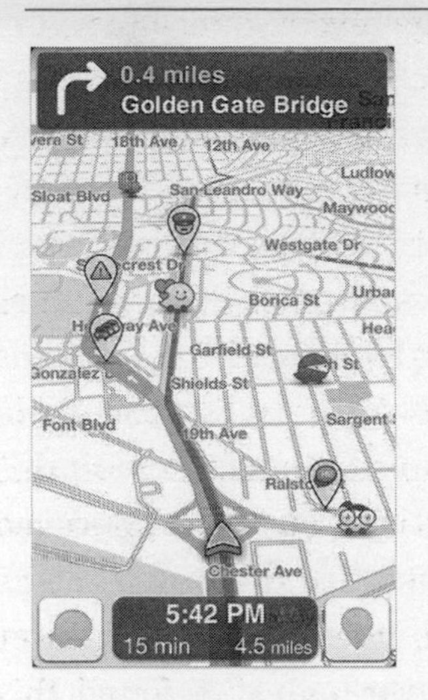

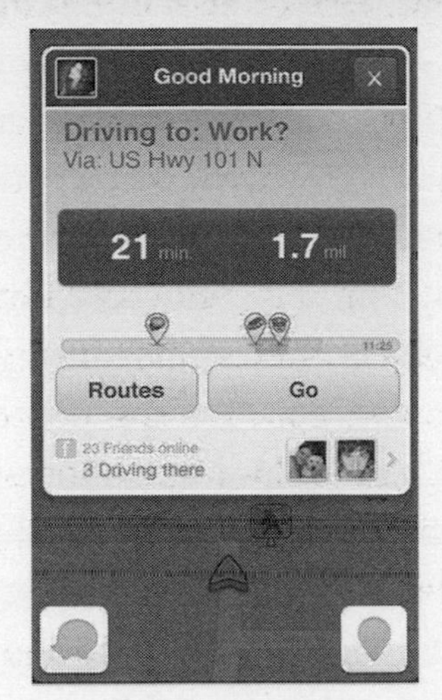

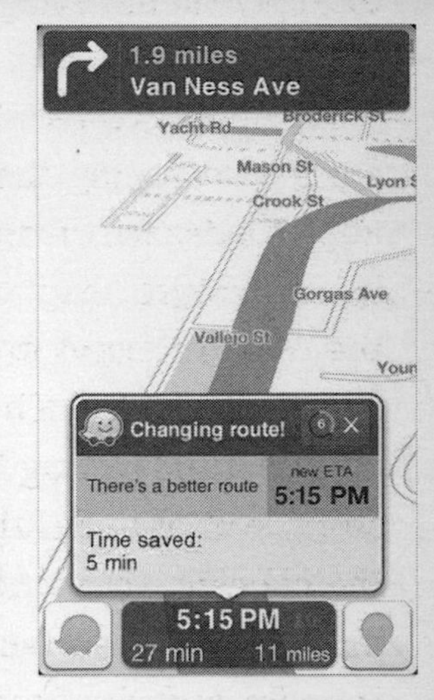

(Courtesy of Waze)

expectations to fulfill. I will forever be up to go see any *Star Wars* film, no matter how bad the reviews are, because I like the universe. I like the emotional associations I have with the way I felt growing up with those films. As a UX designer, I would be able to make my app a part of that story, and I'd have to be extremely sensitive to the look and feel of that world. Any messaging that felt too generic would pull users back down from that magical experience they're expecting.

DON'T BREAK A STORY'S SPELL

Continuity of experience is a factor for many sites and apps. Just as with continuity in film, users don't want you to "break the spell" of the story they're expecting with features or a look and feel that are incongruous. As I've discussed, that was key for me in designing for the *Wall Street Journal*, which readers have a strong bond with and established habits for reading. On top of that desire for continuity, our users came with the expectation of discovery, always hoping to learn something new, as well as the hope for a sense of completeness and of understanding, the assurance that they'll know all the things they need to know. They're looking for peace of mind. For entertainment sites, users may be coming hoping for gossip and pulpy content and looking for that feeling of giddiness that goes along with learning someone's secrets. For those wedding planning sites, users are coming with the warm emotions of being in love and starting out on the exciting new adventure of marriage, but probably also with some anxiety about whether they're going to pull off a great wedding and how much it's going to cost. It's the job of the user experience designer to conjure up these emotions and expectations of users and to make sure the story that the product tells speaks to them.

STORY ISN'T ALL ABOUT THE GRAPHICS

As that Waze screenshot shows so well, the graphics you use are obviously a powerful element of your story, just like the written content, but you should be thinking of all the elements of your product, every interface, as opportunities for storytelling. The technical details of your interface design, such as how you craft your error messages, loading screens, empty pages, alerts, instructions, and forms, all benefit from being a part of the story and keeping the experience up. We have opportunities galore to make our experiences storytelling in style.

The art of film has evolved greatly with the advancement of technology. Most recently 3-D film has been embraced by a number of top filmmakers and guided the creation of their films to the point where directors like Peter Jackson and Alfonso Cuarón urge viewers to see only the 3-D versions because they've crafted the viewing experience specifically to be enjoyed in that way.

So too is the advancement of technology providing UX designers with a wide range of new storytelling tools, from audio features and animation to sensors that allow devices to gather data about where a user is going and what she might be doing, allowing us to tailor experiences accordingly. Several of my students at General Assembly have used these innovations to create experiences that unfold as data about user activity is collected. One of my favorites was a gift-giving app that lets a user send a friend a surprise gift based on the location of the recipient. The story goes like this: User 1 opens the app and picks a friend to receive a gift, and after inputting the friend's mobile phone number, selects a gift to send based on locations near where that friend lives. User 2 gets a text telling her that she has a gift waiting for her and a link to download the app. Once downloaded, the app listens for User 2's location and alerts her with a chime when she's near the store where the gift can be picked up. When the gift is picked up, User 1 gets a confirmation message and User 2 gets a chance to thank her friend. It's a nice beginning, middle, and end story moved forward by technology.

Another great example of the ways designers are making use of new tools to design more engaging interactions is the use of animations on mobile devices. One fun way to do this is in the transitions between screens. I assign my students an article from the website *Smashing Magazine* by innovative designer Rachel Hinman, titled "A New Mobile UX Design Material," which is a great introduction to the kinds of storytelling touches that can be added with animation. Hinman writes that "movement breathes life into everything it touches."[1] A great case of this is the fitness app Moves. It tracks the amount of walking, running, and cycling a user does, evaluating the activity automatically by the user's speed of movement. On the main screen, the app represents each type of activity that day with bubbles of different color whose sizes are proportional to the amount of activity. This is a great way to vividly portray how much more cycling than running you've been doing, for example. But the real magic happens when the user switches to another page that displays a timeline of her activity, so she can see when she is doing each activity during the day. As she switches screens, an animation transforms the bubbles into bars of color along the timeline.

Elements of gamification are another great way to give your products more personality and storytelling quality. I've discussed before how making use of the technique of performative learning developed in gaming is a great way to teach people how to use your site. That's obviously a form of storytelling, following a dictum from fiction writing workshops: "Show, don't tell." But there are other ways to use touches from gaming. A very simple but effective one is LinkedIn's use of a graphic that shows a user how complete her profile is compared to an "expert" level of detail provided. This draws on the device in gaming of telling users how proficient they've become at a game, which was developed to spur them on to reach higher and higher levels of expertise. In LinkedIn it's used to spur them to more fully develop their profiles. I'll discuss some ins and outs of gamification later in the book.

What I hope to show in this chapter is how effective the elements of storytelling that UX designers have to work with are in both enhancing the user experience and guiding the process of designing and getting approvals. When you are presenting an idea to a client or stakeholder, having a story to go along with the mockups you show will make the presentation go a whole lot better. But working with the story in mind every step of the way will also help you spot more opportunities to incorporate storytelling.

SKETCHING AND STORYBOARDING

One of the great myths about those who tell good stories is that they just know how to do it; that they're born storytellers. For sure, storytellers like Dickens, Melville, Kafka, Hemingway, and Kubrick had special talent, but that doesn't mean they didn't have to make all sorts of changes to their work in the process of creating it. The truth is that even the greatest writers revise their work substantially. Artists of all kinds will tell you that their visions for creative projects don't just pop into their minds in some grand moment of insight; they are built up through a development process. That process varies for UX design according to the designer, the company they're working for, and the project, and it's always evolving. But there is a fundamental set of tools for crafting your designs that allow you to test out ideas as you go, get lots of feedback, and only then bring them to polish.

In writing a novel or making a film, the best way to begin is with a rough crafting of the story. For a novel, that's a plot line, which might be crafted in the form of an outline. For a film, it's a storyboard, which includes visuals. UX designers want to use equivalents of both of these to create a site map, a visualization that can be used by the development team to build the interface. You want to go in stages in creating this map, from rough sketches, which let you play around with ideas, to increasingly detailed and polished drawings of pages, up through rough moving prototypes and then a nearly fully functioning prototype, or in some cases an actual fully working prototype with all the bells and whistles.

Taking the place of a plot line are diagrams of your user flows, the routes that users will be able to take through your product, and in place of storyboards are sketches and the more detailed drawings called wireframes, showing varying degrees of detail about the layout and interactions as you proceed through versions. You should always start by sketching out ideas for your page views and the user flows through the site on a whiteboard or on paper. And in this process, you want to be not only plotting out your site, but also making use of all the information you've gathered about users and your understanding of the system you're working with to think creatively about the story you can help craft.

The next diagram is an example of how one of my very rough beginning sketches might look:

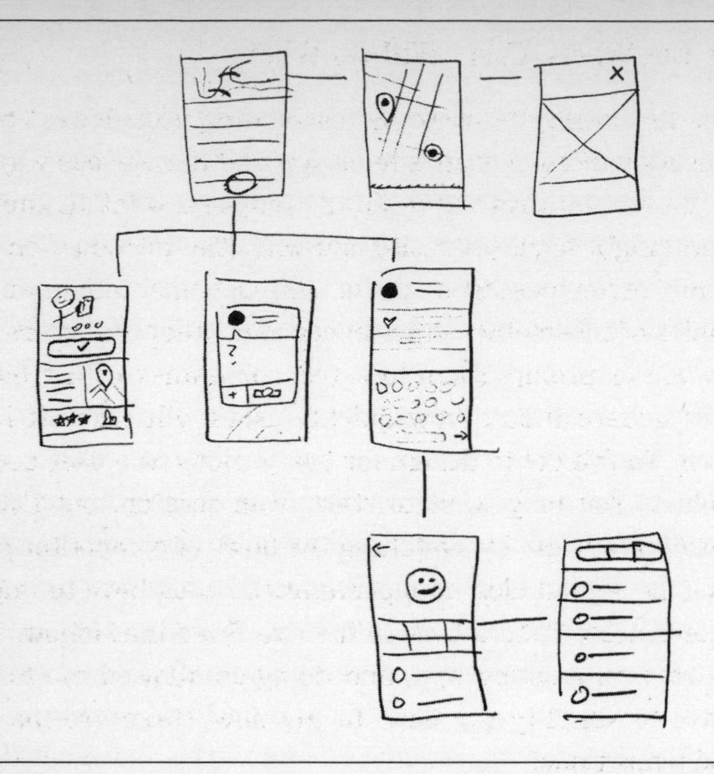

A rough sketch visualizing an app's core task. The quick, disposable nature of sketches allows us to generate several ideas that lend themselves to critique.

When sketching early ideas I especially like to work on graph paper cut to the size of a phone, because I'm designing for mobile, but I've also been known to draw on the back of my unused business cards—they are the perfect ratio of width to height of the screen of a smartphone. There is no shame in drawing on any piece of paper. Some people use notebooks. Even napkins will serve the purpose if an idea comes to you all of a sudden when you don't have anything else handy. You just want to be sure that whatever you choose, you can very easily add, remove, and rearrange the views as you imagine the navigation and core interactions.

Figuring Out Where Users Will Go When

One of the first things to work on is sketching user flows. These map out how users will enter your site or app and the various ways they'll navigate it. As you draw user flows, you also want to think about when users might leave your site and why. The introduction or home page, forms, error messages, alerts, help documentation, and all the other staples of interactive experiences can either pull users along to stay with you or prompt them to leave, sometimes with a bitter feeling. Never underestimate how quickly users will take off if you let them down. You've got to design for every moment a user could leave your product. You may want to start from scratch, but I've always found it useful to begin by sketching the flows of competitor products. That gives me a good idea of opportunities I may have to improve on those experiences. Take a look at the two flows that follow. The first I traced from an existing app, and doing so allowed me to think of many ways to simplify the flow. In my flow, there are many fewer pages and transitions.

Always keep in mind that you want to play the part of a narrator here, and make sure that the product leads users from place to place clearly and never leaves them lost. In a good novel or film, the plot is tightly constructed and all of the story lines work together clearly to drive the story forward, with no plot developments that are confusing or just tangential. With a site or app, of course, we're most often not dealing with a story that moves forward in just one way like a novel or film. Users are free to engage in just about any way they want and roam all around in the order they please. This is why it's essential that in crafting your flows, you make sure users can always navigate easily to core flows and contextual demands of where they want to go next.

For example, users may want to come back to an application after an email or other notification is received. This would mean that you'd want to let them reenter the app sideways, rather than always having to enter from the beginning. Each of the different paths for all

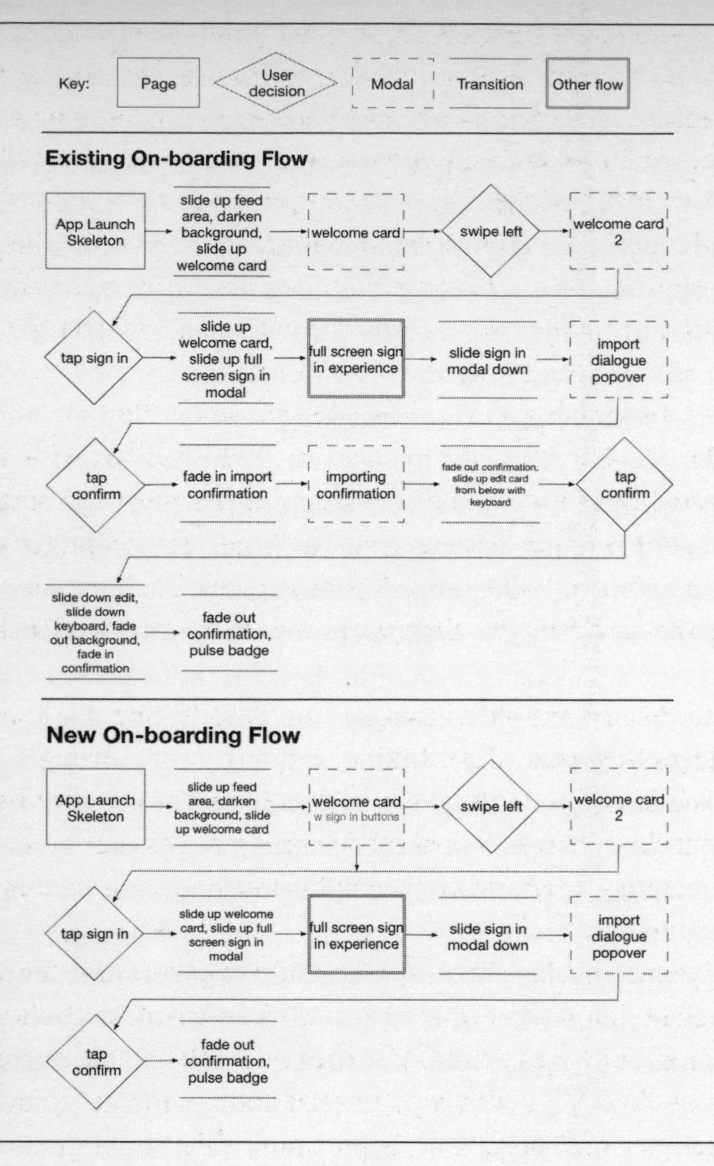

User flows of the first time a user launches an app (onboarding) with pages, user inputs, modals, transitions, and links to other flows. The bottom flow is a proposed simplification of the top flow.

user goals should be thought out to ensure the experience suits every user. This involves putting your personas to use as well as constantly reminding yourself of the business goals. For example, you might want to allow for "power users," people who come to your site all the time and want to go directly to one specific part of it, sidestepping some of the content or more basic navigational UI. But the business you're designing for may require that you not allow bypassing ads or sign-up/sign-in roadblocks, so you'd create some shortcuts for power users but not ones that take them past those.

Much of the emphasis in what you'll read about flows is on enabling user goals, which is the right top priority. But I've learned to make the exercise doubly useful by also seeking out the most opportune junctures for addressing business goals as I go. You want to work any content and features that serve business goals, such as ads and sign-ups, into the parts of the flow users are most strongly incentivized to visit.

I like to discuss an old version of the Spotify flow for the iOS app when addressing this. Just taking a quick read through the flow, you can see it's quite cumbersome. This is one of the real benefits of plotting out flows before you start designing pages; because flows are so abstract, they make overly complicated and long routes through products glaringly clear.

In analyzing this flow, I can spot not only opportunities for making it more efficient, but places where I can work in business goals smoothly and for maximal engagement. For example, take a look at the options menu in the flow. This was a paginated options menu—known in iOS as an action sheet. There is an opportunity there to address the business goal of signing up more subscribers. If you added a "Save for Offline" button there, you would be able to create another opportunity to present browser users with an option to subscribe by adding a pop-up for that when they hit the "Save" button.

In my flows I like to include just about every piece of information that is relevant to the experience, which includes system information; user interactions; animations; any other type of feedback the product

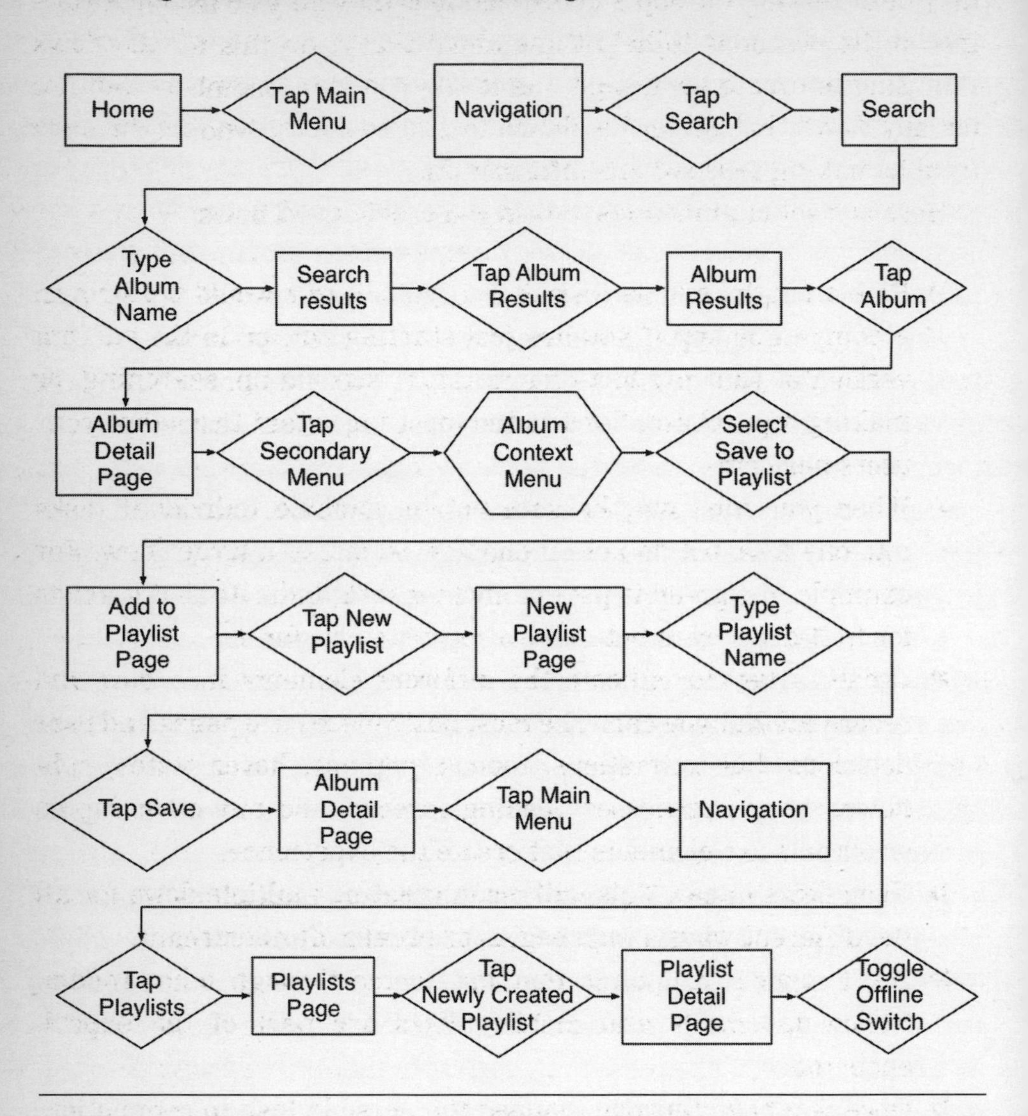

User flow of caching an album for offline listening in an older version of the Spotify iOS app.

gives the user, such as error messages; and the context in which users may be accessing the app and the emotions they may be feeling, drawing on the personas to help think about that. I do this for the flows I'm using to create my design and to show to team members, but not for any flows that might be shown to stakeholders, who might have trouble making sense of this information.

Here is a set of guidelines to help you create good flows:

- Pick a single, simple task that a typical user would perform in a competitor app if you are just starting out, or in the current version of your product—for instance, signing up, searching, or making a purchase. Stick to the most important tasks that your users perform.
- When you start out, be sure not to combine individual tasks into one flow, but do note if one flow is part of a larger flow. For example, if sign-up is part of another task, indicate that it exists for first-time users but make a separate flow for it.
- Create a key to indicate the different elements in a flow and record all that you can. The most basic pieces are pages and user decisions, but animations, menus, pop-ups, hover states, subflows, system processes, loading screens, and any other inputs or outputs are elements that create the experience.
- Keep flows linear. This will mean creating multiple flows for all the different ways a task begins or breaks off midstream.
- Don't neglect endpoints that may come through other media. Follow-up emails and mobile alerts are part of the experience, too.
- Once you have linearly mapped the possible task to completion, identify points where the usability LEMErS come into play by comparing flows. These include number of interactions, number of pages, power user interactions, intelligent uses of data by the system, automated interactions, tips or hints, changes to state based on number of times a task is attempted, and any other heuristic of usability.

» Finally, come back to your flows throughout the design process and compare them as needed based on what you are able to release in each version.

Once you've crafted the basic flows, you should look through them to identify junctures that may cause confusion or irritation, perhaps due to too many steps. You should also look for opportunities to add some storytelling flourishes. I heard a great story about a redesign of the Dallas airport that helps me keep in mind that I should always be on alert for spotting opportunities to tailor flows to the psychology of users and their emotions.

Fliers were complaining that the time spent waiting for baggage was far too long. In response, the powers that be decided the solution was to hire more workers to move the baggage. The complaints dropped, but not nearly enough to indicate that the problem was solved. A consultancy was hired to perform some systems analysis, doing a job similar to that of a UX designer. The consultants went to work by recording the steps it took for a typical customer to make her way through the airport, from when her plane touched down on the tarmac to when she arrived at baggage claim. This is the equivalent of crafting a user flow. They then measured the time required for taxiing to the gate and for each of the following steps. They discovered that it took passengers on average two minutes to walk from the jet bridge to the baggage claim and then eight minutes of waiting for the baggage to arrive. They then took a look at everything about the process that could be changed and that couldn't; the equivalent of learning the constraints of the system. The time for taxiing couldn't be changed, and more workers had already been hired to move the baggage from the plane to the terminal faster, so that wasn't the place to look. What the consultants homed in on was the time customers spent walking from the jet bridge to baggage claim. Their recommendation was to move the jet bridge farther away, which resulted in eight minutes spent walking and just two minutes spent waiting for bags, which led to a significant reduction in customer complaints.

Why did a reversal of the time spent walking and waiting make a difference? The answer lies in a discovery in cognitive psychology about differences in the perception of occupied time versus unoccupied time. The time waiting for baggage was more irritating to people because it was dead time, whereas while they were walking, the time didn't feel wasted.

The solution is directly relevant to UX design. Responding to irritations about a design may not always mean that you should actually make a site or app run faster or make all ads unobtrusive—you'll likely run up against constraints to such changes. You'll often have to look for other ways to improve the experience, maybe with an amusing animated graphic to take up some of the wait time. Also keep in mind that changes in flow can be irritating to users, even if you see advantages to the new way. If you're working on an existing product and adding a new page or feature to it or doing a redesign, user flows can give you an idea of what users will be expecting based on their past experiences on the site. Going back to the story of my attempt to introduce the pull-to-refresh/swipe-to-skip interaction in the WSJ Live app, I was disregarding an important feature of the user flow. The swipe-to-skip may have become an increasingly familiar feature, but it cut against the grain of the way users tended to navigate the site.

This is made very clear by taking a look at these two flows next to each other:

Once you've worked out your flows, it's time to start crafting the pages, and just as filmmakers use rough storyboards to plot out their shoots, you want to first focus on the smaller units of your story, again starting with sketches and then working up to wireframes, the full-page schematics that begin to connect the underlying information architecture of your flows with the design of the navigations and interactions.

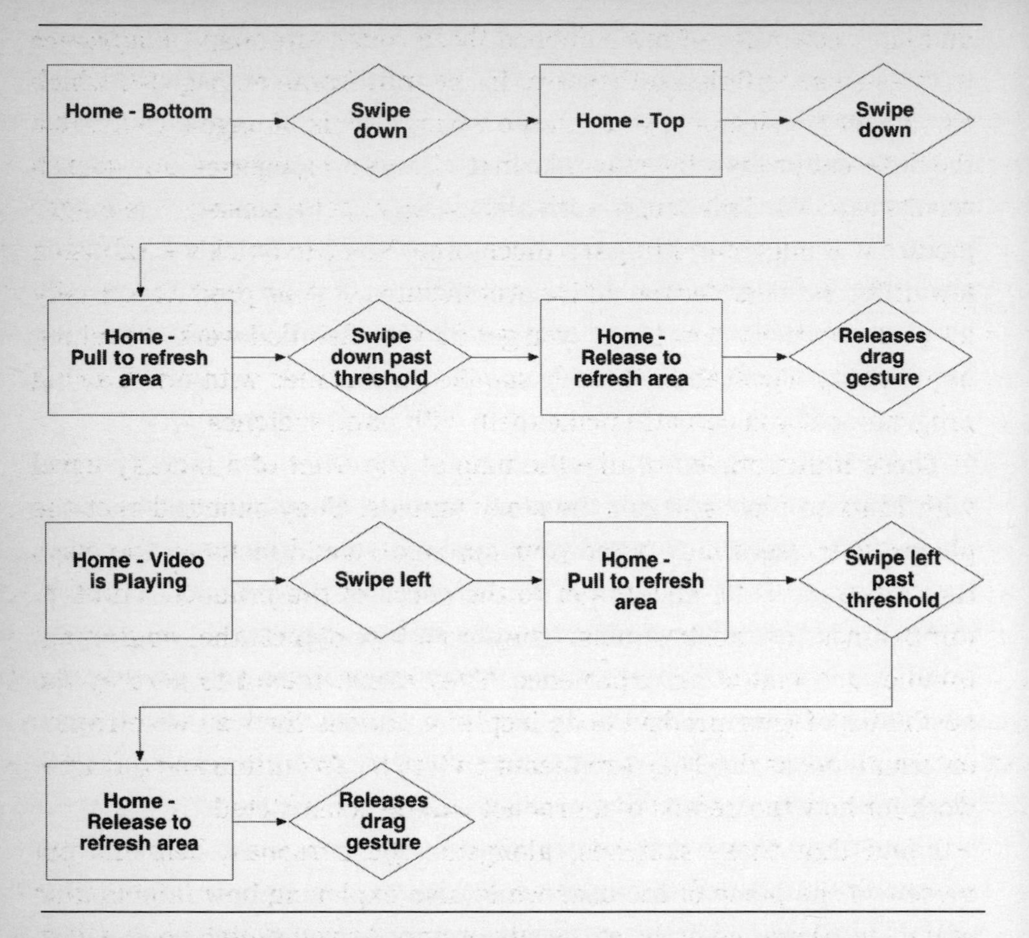

Top: User flow of pull-to-refresh in Twitter. Begins at the bottom because of the reverse-chronologically ordered feed. Note that the user is already performing the gesture to refresh. Bottom: User flow of pull-to-refresh in WSJ Live. User must know that this gesture is possible because no other one precedes it.

Start with Quick and Dirty Miniframes

In putting the sketches for pages together, creating a site map, I suggest also working very much in the rough at first. A former student and later coworker of mine dubbed these rough site maps *miniframes* to stress how unfinished they are. In the miniframe on page 96, which I made for a video app, you can see various kinds of page layouts, like the different forms a list may take in the browse, categories, and search results screens. This rough work allows you to get a sense of the bigger picture without committing too much time. You can quickly establish a few different ideas for the entire architecture of your product to really let your creativity flow before you get into the detailed work of making high-fidelity wireframes. I made sample miniframes with my drawing program, but you can also make them with hand sketches.

These miniframes are like the map at the front of a fantasy novel with hints to places where the story unfolds. They should depict the places your users may enter your app and should focus on the ways those users will be able to get to the cores of the product. Think of miniframes as abstractions; they roughly depict the beginning, middle, and end of an experience. They aren't meant to portray the aesthetics of your product or to inspire emotions the way wireframes or visual mocks do. They are meant only to be an outline and a framework for how the details of a product will be constructed.

I find that these sketches, alongside the personas, help me put myself in the place of the user while also exploring how information will move along the paths of the site or app. As you sketch your pages, you want to put them in the order of the flows so that they really do work as a map. This helps you spot places where information may be blocked off from the people who want to use it; one of the real tricks of crafting site maps is that users and the information they want are not always in the same place at once. For example, you may want to have a page that combines videos with the biographical information about a presenter that you might have planned for a separate page.

Your site map will also help you understand how well you're taking account of the system issues, such as the time for calls to the databases on the servers. And you want to represent this information on the views. This rough map can also be a way to prioritize your and the rest of your team's work and establish an architecture for engineering

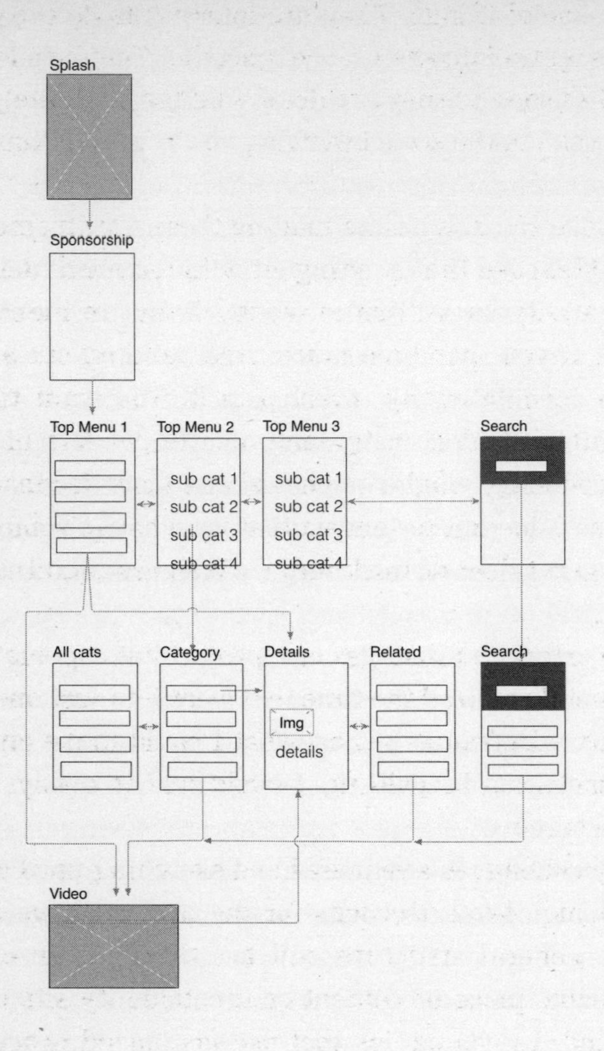

Miniframes for a video application

work to begin. You don't want to keep your sketches close to the vest; you want to begin getting feedback about them early. As I'll discuss more in chapter 5, you never know who on your team may have good ideas for you or see problems you're overlooking.

In his book *Sketching the User Experience*, Bill Buxton says, "Sketches are social things. They are lonely outside the company of other sketches and related reference material. They are lonely if they are discarded as soon as they are done. And they definitely are happiest when everyone in the studio working on the project has spent time with them."[2]

I used to spend too much time making these miniframes, but after about a year, I learned that starting off with too much detail is a hindrance to creativity as well as to feedback, not to mention being a big time suck. If you spend too much time building out a single concept, you can become overly invested in it. You want to be free to give lots of different ideas a try and also to get lots of ideas from your team. Producing rough sketches elicits more feedback, because people aren't so reluctant to suggest that you change something if you haven't put a great deal of work into it. Sketches facilitate free-form ideation.

Time is important in all stages of a project but especially so at the beginning. When I realized the time that went into just one set of even medium-fidelity wireframes versus what I could make on paper with simple hand sketching in a sitting, I made sure to always spend time away from the screen.

Many of my colleagues swear by hand sketching until a number of the important high-level decisions for the product have been made, like what the general structure will be, the number of pages, or whether a specific piece of content or functionality sits on the front end or back end. In companies that use fast-paced processes, product teams may never even make wireframes, and these sketches will stand in for the wires for the visual designers to begin working.

These days, when sketching my pages I use an approach I read about on the website Boxes and Arrows that starts with the cores of an experience, the central pieces that will be interacted with the most. If you're designing an app for downloading and reading books, the core pages would be those for searching for books and for reading them. If you're working on an e-commerce site, the cores would be the product display pages and the purchase page. If the core for your product isn't obvious, then think through where users will spend the most time. If you're working on a redesign or a new product that's closely related to another one you have access to information about, you can mine the usage data to determine this. There is also a host of domain knowledge for many types of products, such as informational, entertainment, and educational experiences you can tap into by speaking with experts in the field. I've turned to colleagues in editorial teams numerous times to better understand issues around business and finance news. Without expert input I could have missed vital parts to a core task.

Progressing to Wireframes

Along with user research, wireframing is the bread and butter of a UX designer's work as she is starting out. In fact, many jobs may only define UX deliverables as wireframes. That gives you an opportunity to set the record straight, however. Any employer who asks only for wireframes from a UX designer does not understand what goes into creating a great experience. But that said, wires are at the heart of the process. These more formal, more detailed drawings are important for the UX designer in wrestling with every little interaction and screen change dynamic, and also for showing to the visual design team, the development team, and often the stakeholders higher up (though stakeholders can be hard to understand, so, as we'll discuss, it's a good idea to create other types of depictions for them).

The tool I use to create my wireframes is OmniGraffle, which is a wonderful program. It's Mac only, though, so you should consider using Balsamiq Mockups if you work on a PC. Both of these tools provide the invaluable feature of stencils for every kind of interface element you can think of; all the sorts of windows, buttons, icons, tabs, headings, ad units, and so on. A designer named Michael Angeles, who actually works for Balsamiq, developed my favorite stencil set

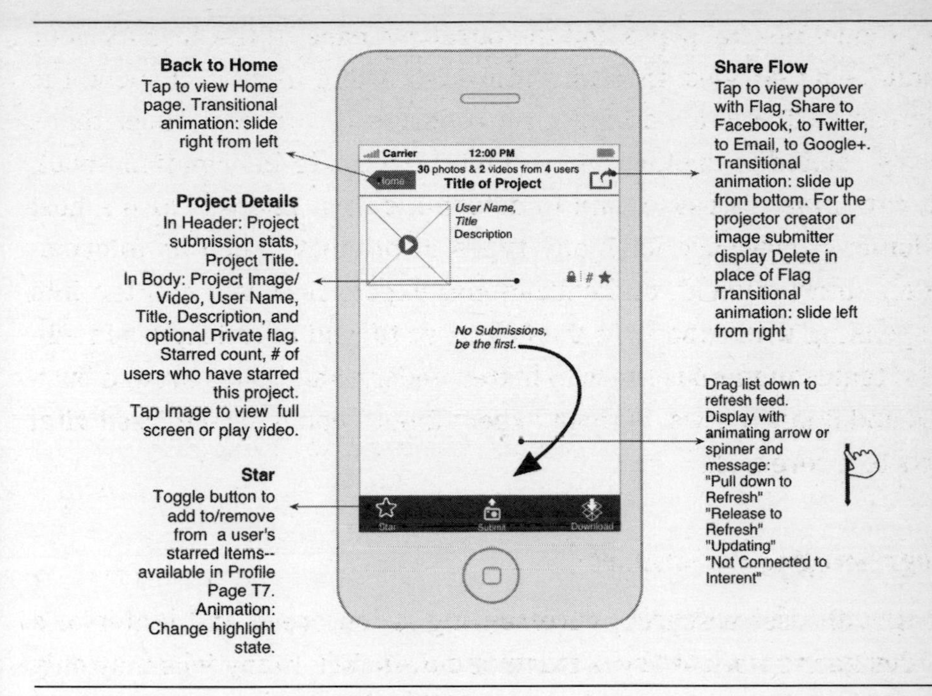
Back to Home
Tap to view Home page. Transitional animation: slide right from left
Project Details
In Header: Project submission stats, Project Title.
In Body: Project Image/ Video, User Name, Title, Description, and optional Private flag. Starred count, # of users who have starred this project.
Tap Image to view full screen or play video.
Star
Toggle button to add to/remove from a user's starred items-- available in Profile Page T7. Animation: Change highlight state.
Carrier
12:00 PM
30 photos & 2 videos from 4 users
Title of Project
User Name,
Title
Description
No Submissions, be the first.
Share Flow
Tap to view popover with Flag, Share to Facebook, to Twitter, to Email, to Google+. Transitional animation: slide up from bottom. For the projector creator or image submitter display Delete in place of Flag Transitional animation: slide left from right
Drag list down to refresh feed. Display with animating arrow or spinner and message: "Pull down to Refresh" "Release to Refresh" "Updating" "Not Connected to Interent"

Full wireframe for a photo application

to use, which is a stock set in OmniGraffle 6. Stencils let you drag and drop interface elements onto blank pages quickly. Even at this stage, I typically like to make three or four versions of one potential idea so that I can again solicit feedback from my team or even from users. Wires help to clarify features and how interactions and flows will work, and you don't want to set them in stone right away. Keep in mind that if you're showing wires at early stages, you should indicate clearly to those you show them to what you're looking for feedback about—for example, if you've included only your basic layout, be sure to ask them to comment only on that. Otherwise advice can go off on tangents that aren't helpful.

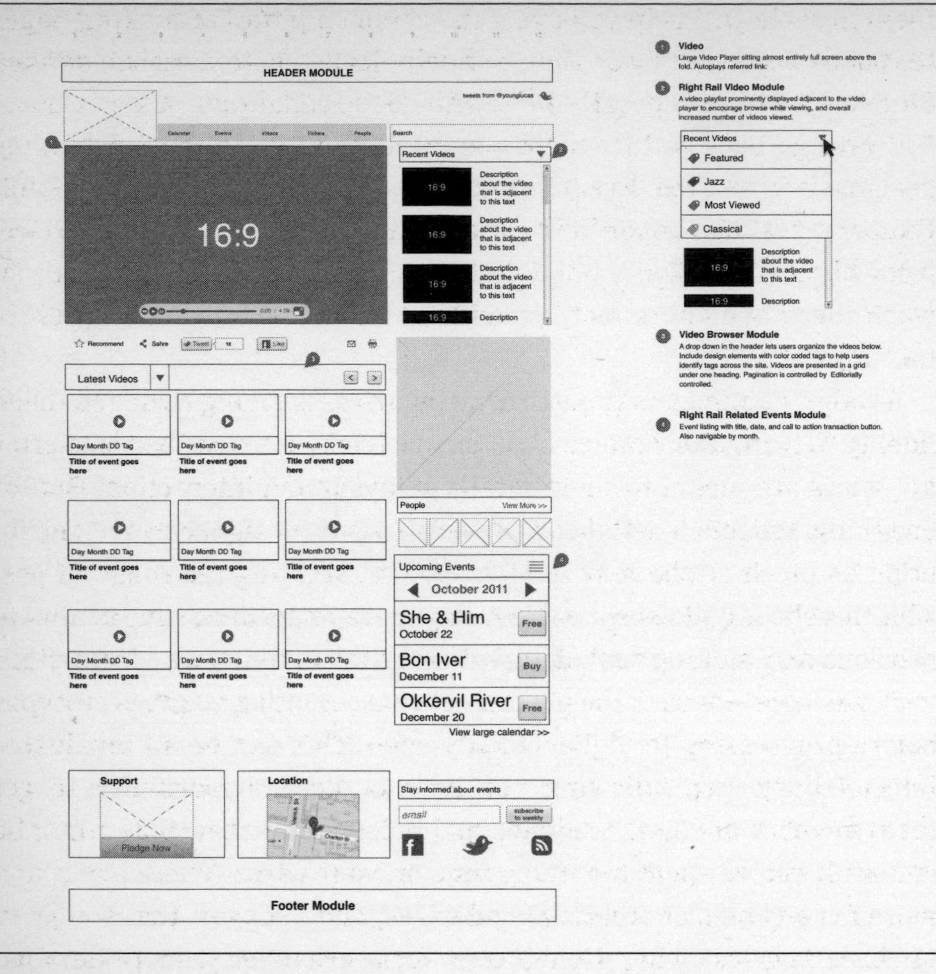

Full wireframe for a video website

The two most common mistakes I see my students make in beginning to draw wires are not working to the actual scale of the screen the product will display on and including unnecessary interface elements. Just because your wires won't be the final design doesn't mean you shouldn't be concerned with proper widths and heights. Drawing them to scale will help you avoid the common pitfall of making pages that don't read well when they're finally loaded onto a mobile screen. Simplicity will also greatly help with good readability. A great quote I always go back to that helps me avoid putting too much UI in my designs is from the French aviator and writer Antoine de Saint-Exupéry, best known for his beloved children's book *The Little Prince*, from his memoir *Wind, Sand and Stars*: "Perfection is achieved not when there is nothing more to add but when there is nothing left to take away."[3]

Another common mistake in drawing wires is giving them too much fidelity. Getting the balance right can be tricky for sure, because after all, wires are meant to show details of layout and interaction. But for one thing, too much detail can prevent a visual designer from contributing as much as she may have to offer by limiting the range of possibilities she might consider. Probably more important, time is always precious and making such detailed wires takes time away from other very valuable stages of the process, such as creating rough prototypes before progressing to higher-fidelity ones. This can be an invaluable intermediary step, allowing you another great opportunity to get team member and user feedback and to iterate further, that might be cut out if you've spent too much time on your wires. There are many more ins and outs of creating good wires, and I suggest that you go to Michael Angeles's blog, Konigi.com, for a great set of more detailed insights and a wide range of wireframe samples.

In most cases, you'll need to get approval of your wires before you proceed to prototyping.

MAKING A DESIGN MOVE

Prototyping is all about getting a good feel for how a product will actually perform if it's built as you've designed it. Functioning prototypes are vital for testing how interactions will actually be used and for interpreting user feedback through the usability LEMErS—how learnable, efficient, memorable, error-free, and overall satisfying the product really is. The biggest difference between wires and prototypes is motion, and that is such a large part of what sets digital products apart that to not take advantage of the opportunity to see your design actually in motion before you complete it would be a travesty. Don't shy away; it's also lots of fun.

I have found prototyping to be the most creative and enjoyable part of my job. Toiling away on making an interactive model and then testing it with users is at the very heart of UX, and the benefits in time and money saved in the actual building of the product are enormous. That doesn't mean that all prototypes have to be time-consuming to create, or even have a great degree of fidelity to the look and feel of a product. Don't think of prototypes as simply the fulfillment of your design, the translation of it into an interactive model. Think of them as part of the process of crafting your design.

I make two basic kinds of prototypes, for different purposes. The first is an interactive prototype, which I use for getting feedback from my team and for user testing, and most often includes only limited visual design. The second is actually a video showing how the product will work, which I use for stakeholder reviewers and which is created in collaboration with the visual design team.

Interactive Prototypes

In making the first type, once again I suggest that you start with quick and dirty versions, get feedback from your team about them, and do user testing with them early on. It used to be that developers had to make prototypes, because designers didn't know how to program, and many designers still don't. But many prototyping tools have now been developed that allow anyone to begin making interactive prototypes in a snap.

I strongly recommend that you follow the practice of rapid prototyping, testing several versions of rough prototypes of smaller units of your design, rather than starting with a full prototype. I often begin my prototyping by creating a testable version of just a single interaction. I again start with the core, with the most commonly performed inter-

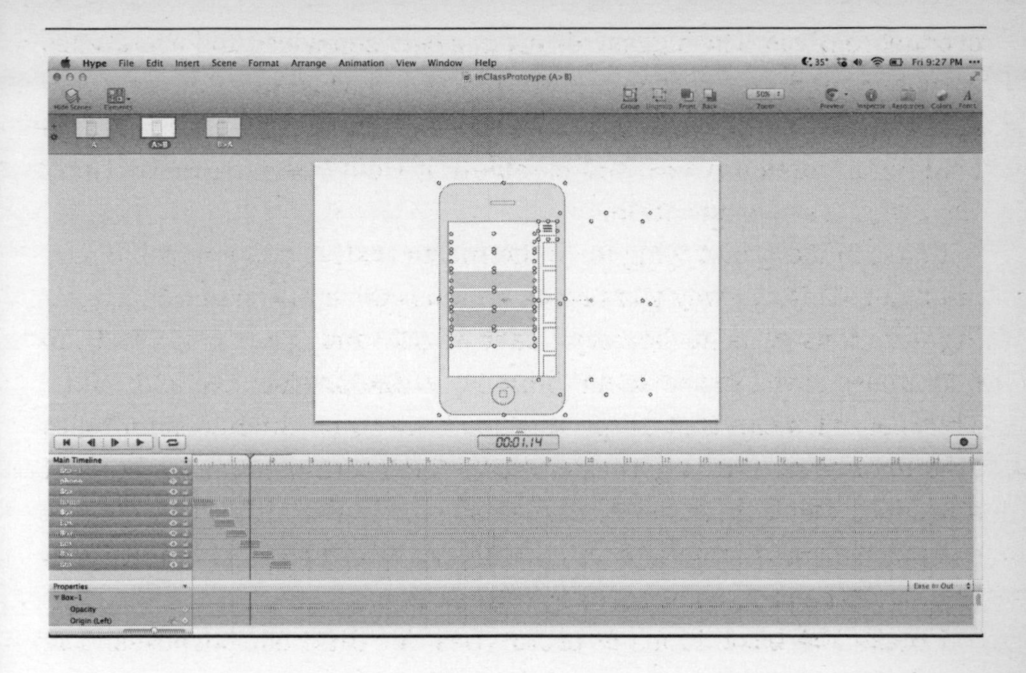

A screenshot of Tumult Hype and a prototype. The lower portion of the software shows animations on a timeline. Using Hype you can trigger animations, like transitions, by assigning actions to the UI elements in the upper stage portion.

actions. Beginning this way, just for yourself at first, almost always helps you discover changes you want to make before anyone else is involved at all. But such rough prototypes have also proven extremely helpful to me in getting feedback early enough from my team and from users. I've gotten some pushback from product managers on user tests that don't include visual design, because they think users won't really understand the look and feel of a product, but the alternatives of either not testing or waiting for visual design before testing can mean mistakes and time wasted on corrections. To contend with the issue that the prototypes are so rough, I recommend stressing to your test subjects and your team that the prototypes are not indicative of the final visuals or performance of the product, and limiting them to testing of particular parts of your designs, rather than getting an overall assessment of a product. So, for example, you can use the rough prototypes to test how people rank three different navigations from your home page to a few of the next screens they could progress to.

A number of tools for fast and rough prototyping are now on the market. One of them, an iOS app called POP (for Prototyping on Paper) lets you take photos of your sketches and string them together, allowing you to prototype with only pen, paper, and an iPhone. Other tools for easy prototyping exist, such as InVision, Axure, and Flinto, but the big improvements over these others that POP offers is actually putting the pages on a device and adding animations to them. I create multiple rough interactive prototypes with low-fidelity sketched assets to evaluate early navigation models that come from sets of miniframes. The lower fidelity the prototype, the more discerning you must be with whom you select to test the prototypes. At the lowest level you must use objective judgment to categorize your hypothesis about user behavior. At the highest fidelity—with near final visual assets, interactivity, and motion—you can test on varying segments of your actual user population.

Motion Prototypes

The second type of prototypes I make, the video versions, are based on my designs, but they're not interactive; in truth, they are pure fiction. They are wonderfully creative, but ultimately they are art, existing to elicit questions, and at times closely similar to the pitches that advertising agencies present to clients. They're a high-fidelity visualization of the product story. That doesn't mean you won't make changes to your design after showing them; never think of any kind of prototype as a finished model. In fact, these videos have been very useful in product development. The designers of Google Glass, for one, made great use of them, creating video simulations of what users would see on the small screen affixed to the glasses as they walked around, such as competitive product information if they were walking through a store or the names of people approaching them, which would be very helpful for those awkward moments when we can't put a name to a face.

But I've also found that these video prototypes are especially helpful in getting approvals to go ahead with a design.

STAKEHOLDERS AND THE SIXTH FINGER

As I discussed earlier, storytelling not only makes for a richer user experience, but it can be instrumental in getting your work approved, and also in creating a work culture that is more attuned to user experience concerns. The single biggest complaint I've heard from my students about actually practicing UX on the job is, "My boss just keeps descoping all the most important parts of the experience."

I've felt this same thing many times in my own work, and I've told some stories already in this book about my experiences with it. Sometimes our ideas are shot down for good reasons—maybe they're just too innovative. I don't mind features being removed then, because I've probably gotten away from thinking about what the user really wants and needs. But sometimes the feature being nixed is a component that affects the core usability. No matter; the people in charge of approvals are still totally free to overrule you.

This can make it tempting to resort to subterfuge.

I'll never forget the time a senior designer told me a story of the sixth finger. It was at the *Wall Street Journal*, where we had a stakeholder known for always getting his way. His opinions were unmovable, and they often clashed with what we wanted to do. One tactic we used was to give him options to try to steer his decision-making. People had competing theories about the best way to do this: Do you put the best option last, so that you end the presentation with a eureka moment for him, or do you put it first to try to set a positive tone for the review? None seemed to work very well.

Then one day I was preparing a review with a more senior designer. I had designed three options for a navigation model, one of which we felt was the clear winner, and made simple wireframes to show them. To my surprise, when I showed my wireframes to my colleague, he took a pen and started to draw in the rest of the interface that the navigation was a part of. "We're painting the king a sixth finger," he said. I had no idea what he was talking about. He explained, "In dealing with a tyrant king, you want to distract his attention from any real issues by supplying him with fake ones." If he sees a sixth finger—the obvious mistake—he won't pay attention to something else going on with the first five. When the day of the review came, we got plenty of feedback from "the tyrant," but it was all about our layout. The navigation made it through unscathed. The sixth finger had worked!

You don't really want to have to resort to this (though you might want to try it sometimes). Much better is to tell a really good story to stakeholders.

Video prototypes are a great way of doing this. They provide a richer visual experience of your design than either flat wireframes or even more high-fidelity prototypes often can. Many people who don't make wireframes find them very hard to follow, and there's nothing at all engaging about them. By contrast, a product video can be filled with emotion and fictional content, allowing stakeholders to actually have some of the experience you're promising.

Both types of prototype represent the nexus of all your research and drawing, and once you progress to creating the higher-fidelity versions that you'll most often want to use for testing with users, they should include thoughts around content strategy, information architecture, interface and interaction design, and animations. These higher-fidelity versions take longer to make, but I think they're worth the effort, because when using a prototype for user testing, the closer you can get the look and feel to the actual product, the more reliable your results will be.

I use two tools for hi-fi interactive prototypes, Tumult Hype and InVision, but not simultaneously. I use Hype for motion prototypes or interactive ones that need to display custom animations. InVision is good for linking together screens, but not for customization, so it doesn't work for showing the custom animations I often create.

A PICTURE IS WORTH A THOUSAND WORDS, BUT WORDS COUNT TOO

A chapter on storytelling can't fail to address the words we write in UX. It is debatable who should be in charge of writing copy. Almost everyone involved likes to have a say, but interactive and educational copy is the province of the UX designer. If it isn't thought of as part of UX, then it will likely be simply layered onto a design, not made a part of the experience, and bad word choices may go untested.

One key thing to keep in mind is that the text used is not only doing the work of instructing users, it's also an element of a product's branding. The tone of your copy should be carefully considered, representing the tone of your product. Whimsical language is great for a fun or kid-oriented app, but a more serious tone should be used for a hard news product. Settling on the perfect wording choices can be agonizing, because even a very small snafu in wording can lead to big problems. But that's one reason why the copy deserves the same amount of attention, if not more, than other polishes.

When I speak about copy being part of the experience and not a layer on top of it, I mean that quite literally. Overlays that teach users about the interface have the opposite effect of what they are intended for, in my experience.

My war on overlays started while I was working at the *Wall Street Journal*. One of the editors at the *Journal* snuck in text over many elements of the design for the video app explaining their functions or how to use them, such as how to open an article by clicking on it and what various icons meant. He even included one bit that told users what overlay tips were and how to close them. As I said before, sometimes such expedience is better than leaving some users confused, but I have to say that this last one of his sent me over the edge. I jokingly made an overlay to show him that pointed at pictures with

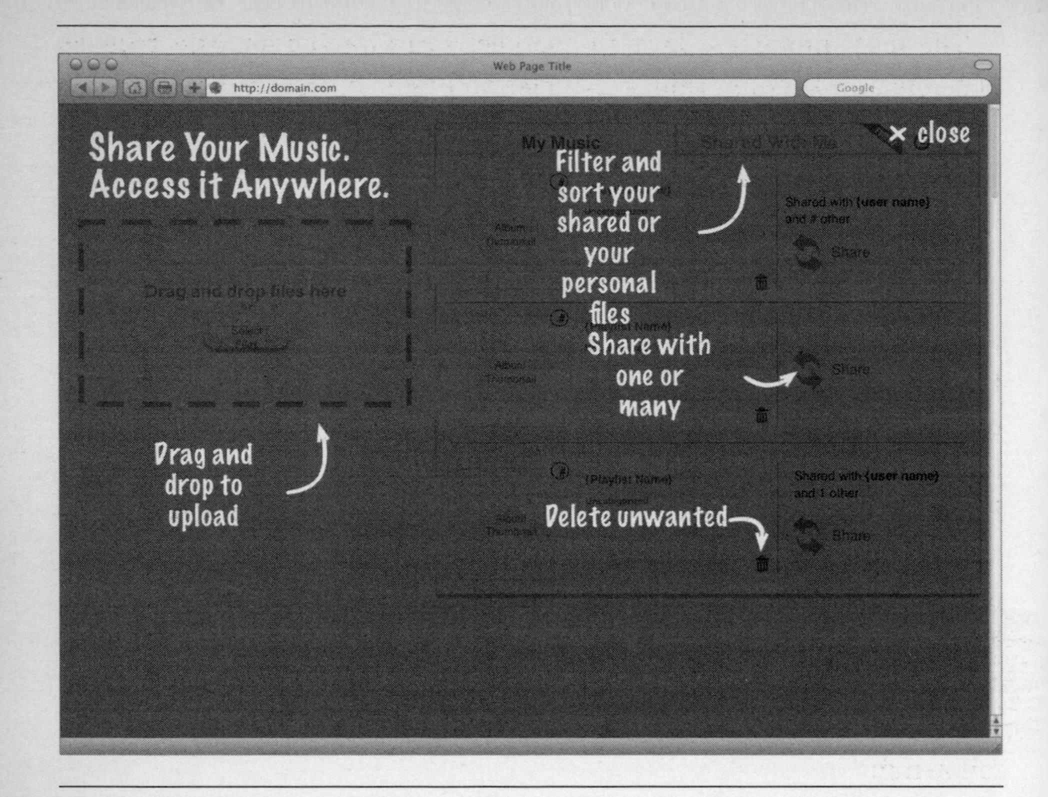

Coachmarks ask users to learn things they may not need immediately and make up for user interface elements that are confusing. Instead, try to find UI that is clear or show coachmarks only when they are needed, and not all at once up front.

instructions on how to look at them with the eyes, how text should be read left to right, and what a question mark was. He wasn't especially amused.

These overlays are often a sign of bad UX design. If the editor really thought that users wouldn't know how to interact with the interface, then there was a problem with the interface. And if it's unavoidable that an interface requires some explanation, then it should be done more thoughtfully.

The most important keys to good copy are having as little copy as possible and keeping things as brief as possible. User flows can help identify where copy is needed, but I suggest testing various possibilities to discover where interactions are intuitive and where pointers and other messaging are needed. Is a walkthrough needed up front, or will signaling functionality through button labels, tool tips, and confirmations along the way suffice? Are icons conveying their utility clearly by themselves, or are they confusing and so need a label? Can a visual alone be used to indicate an error in entering some data, or do you need a message to pop up? All such copy issues should be tested, and in my experience, every detail of copy should be included in tests. A button that says "Save" versus "Done" or "Cancel" versus "Close" may make a substantial difference in user comprehension. Just about any copy is subject to interpretation.

No rules will cover every eventuality or take the place of this testing, but the gurus at the Nielsen Norman Group have issued a great set of guidelines about what to shoot for in copy that include the following:

- **Consistency and standards:** Help not only with language the platforms are already using but also with placement of labels.
- **Visibility of system status:** Indicate where users are, where they are going, or what their interactions have just done.
- **Match between system and the real world:** Use the language of your users so confusion is minimized or eliminated altogether.

Also keep in mind that visual designers can play an important role in copywriting by making typography selections and design choices that help draw users' attention to the right places.

HOW DO YOU TELL SOMEONE THEY'VE MESSED UP?

One particular category of copywriting you need to think carefully about is the writing of error messages. Of course, steering users away from making errors in navigating or performing functions is a key component of user experience design, but some user errors are just about inevitable no matter how good a design is. People are sure to mistype their credit card information sometimes or fail to fill in or check some of the required boxes. And some links that come up in searches will be to pages that are no longer available. You've got to plan for such issues and write explanations that are not annoying to users, who will already be at least a little irritated that something's gone wrong.

First of all, messages must be perfectly clear about how to resolve the problem. You don't always need to use language to show users the error of their ways. The OSX user login on a Mac is a great example. When a user enters the wrong password, the text box shakes horizontally and highlights the incorrectly entered password as if to say no by shaking its "head." And on top of that, when a user begins retyping the password, the incorrect one is automatically erased; the user doesn't have to blank the box out. If you do have to use words, try to make them empathetic or maybe even amusing. One good case of this is a message in Google Chrome, "The following page(s) have become unresponsive. You can wait for them to become responsive or kill them," which comes along with two tabs, one for "Kill" and one for "Wait." That message tells a great empathetic story: we know what an unbelievable pain it is that things that were once on the limitless, always-at-your-fingertips World Wide Web, and which you've been led to believe still are, have for some perverse reason gone missing.

Of course, even when you've taken all of this care in crafting and recrafting a design, and even as compelling as your stakeholders may find it, users may still have problems with it. Prototyping helps discover and prevent this, but an important part of UX is verifying the quality of the experience you've created with user testing. We've got a great set of tools for doing so, and that's the subject of the next chapter.

POINTS TO REMEMBER

Interface Designs Are the Facial Expressions of Digital Products

- Think of yourself as a storyteller. Always be looking for ways to add touches of drama and delight to your design in order to make it entertaining and emotionally engaging.
- The brand elements and content you're given are only some of the components of the product's story; the interface design, the user flow design, your selection of other graphics, and even the design of icons and buttons and the text of labels contribute to the story.
- Every story has a genre, and you must understand how the type of product you're designing and the users you're targeting dictate the way you should tell your story.
- Articulating the story of your product will both guide your every step in creating your design and make your case for it more persuasive to stakeholders you need to get buy-in from.
- Carefully consider the emotions your users will be bringing with them and those they want your product to evoke for them, and always remember that the experience users want from different types of products, say e-commerce versus hard news, will vary widely.
- While traditional stories unfold in only one way, users of digital products are free to make their own way, so you must craft user flows to take into account all the different routes users may want to take and their different points of entry. Always carefully consider that users can leave your product at any time; you never want to frustrate them so account for "sideways" exit and entry to a flow.

(continued)

- Craft your pages beginning with rough sketches, always keeping your flows and personas at hand and factoring in systems information.
- When drawing your wireframes, create them to the scale of the device you're designing for and don't make them so detailed that they prevent the visual designer from contributing creative ideas.
- In creating prototypes, start with quick and dirty versions and get the early feedback of your team and of users. For stakeholders, consider creating video prototypes in order to provide a richer visual experience.
- Make sure all copy you write, even for the most basic labels, optimizes opportunities to delight, and in general design for as little copy as possible.

Chapter 4

INNOVATION IS NOT FOR INNOVATION'S SAKE

When describing a product as having great UX, users and creators tend to be on the same page. They both use words like delightful, intuitive, and fun. The feeling of a product that's not only easy to use but actually pleasurable, is perfectly clear to both. Not so when it comes to innovation. While creators tend to be intent on innovating, users are often much less enthusiastic. Some users are always looking for new things and don't mind having to learn in general. But often when an existing product changes, its loyal users are disgruntled about having to relearn a task they could already perform. Innovation generally gets a bad rap if the changes made don't actually improve the experience or if there is neither any real need nor any true desire for the new features or product.

One of the best things about working with web and software products is that innovation is at the very core of the business; it's what enables us to make existing products even more successful, and it allows us to invent whole new types of products. Innovation often gives a product an edge over the competition. And if companies don't keep innovating they risk falling prey to the danger Harvard Business

School professor Clayton Christensen pinpointed in his influential book *The Innovator's Dilemma*. If you don't adopt the better, faster, smarter way to offer your service, someone else will. Just look at the competition that payment service PayPal has been facing from companies like Square, Braintree, and Venmo. PayPal may have solved its dilemma temporarily by purchasing those last two companies, but the mandate to keep innovating isn't about to abate.

If that were the only issue with innovation—that you've got to keep doing it—maybe it wouldn't be so hard to get right. What makes innovation so tricky is that it can easily backfire, driving users back to something familiar. This double-edged-sword aspect of innovation is one of the biggest challenges a UX designer contends with, but also one of the most satisfying.

I love that helping to make sure cutting-edge new products are easy to use and pleasing are big parts of the job. You're a key player in helping people on the path to the future of everyday computer interactions, and there's always so much to be discovering and trying out because the target is always moving. This also means you have a lot of responsibility. When you get it right, you're redefining the meaning of a positive experience. New technologies regularly allow us to introduce users to new solutions and features they couldn't have told you they wanted. Using GPS sensors to automatically fill in a starting point for getting directions, remembering the position in a video when a user stops midway, suggesting more content when a user reaches the end of a page, mimicking the flip of a page in a gesture-based reading app, placing an unknown feature in the path of a known one (pull-to-refresh) to yield discoverability, opening the world of publishing up to the masses with blogs and social media, consolidating the world's music to create automated radio stations—no one asked for these features, but now that they're here we don't want to live without them.

And the simple fact is that we have no choice but to innovate. Innovation is either something you introduce or something you make up for. If you're not doing it, sooner or later your competitors will be.

My career has coincided with the rise of mobile, and as a fan and student of novel human-computer interactions, that's where I made my path. Every product I've worked on since graduate school has had to deal with the transition to mobile. It can be hard to remember what a huge change this was for interaction design because users no longer had a mouse, and then the keyboard also went away on most devices. Even at a legacy company like the *Wall Street Journal* we had to make the move early. Mobile devices were a high-end product and we knew most *Journal* readers would be snapping them up. So we had to dive into making apps. Innovation happened to us. It was a great time to be making things for the newspaper industry because the news business was so in flux and I was in the thick of it, sailing into uncharted waters.

One of the most interesting lessons I learned from being in the first wave of an innovative technology washing over an older industry was how readily users generally adapt after the first tumult of adoption. But that said, bringing them through the transition can be treacherous, and every UX designer should be highly aware of how difficult it can be to anticipate users' desires and reactions, and of how many new products fail. Just take a look at the user reviews in any app store and you'll get a shock to the system. I cannot express the depths of uselessness that one-star reviews that say just "This sucks" have for me in terms of figuring out how to make improvements, but they sure do speak loudly, and I can't believe how many of them I see across app stores.

This is why it's so important to understand why you're introducing an innovation and exactly what the advantage of it is for the user, which is true for both changes to existing products and the introduction of entirely new ones. It's also why user testing is so important. Even if you've got good answers about the value being added, users may not be ready for the change or able to see the value without an assist from you. In this chapter, I'm first going to explore some of the especially knotty issues with innovation and some helpful rules of the road, and then I'll cover the methods of user testing that I've found the most efficient and fruitful in helping me decide when and how to innovate and how to ease users through the change.

TAKING WORK AWAY

One of the few reliable rules in innovation is that it is rarely described positively by users unless it takes work away. I'll call this *innovation by removal*, though in fact it often involves adding technology to your product. The online food ordering company Seamless is a good example. It's generated a good following by removing the annoying and time-consuming inconsistency in the experience of ordering food for delivery. If you do any takeout ordering, you'll know that online menu displays and ways of navigating them and placing orders are all over the map, and they're often cumbersome to use. On Seamless, each restaurant's menu has been put into a consistent design, and all of them can be interacted with in the same way. In addition, users' payment information is saved, so after your initial order, placing a new one is a snap. Another great example is the mobile app Uber, which has simplified the huge hassle of hailing a cab. I live in New York City and there are times when getting a taxi can be nearly impossible—and that's always right when you need to get somewhere fast. By using GPS location technology, Uber matches the location of users with that of taxis nearby, so you know where to head.

Other products use recent innovations in hardware to remove the hassle of data entry, such as the Chrome browser's autofill feature, which immediately fills in first and last names, phone numbers, email addresses, home addresses, and other key information whenever it's requested. Dropbox is a great case of using the big new innovation of cloud data storage services in a way that has removed a big hassle. Moving data between devices and sharing it with others used to require all sorts of intermediaries, going way back to floppy disks and up to flash drives. Now with Dropbox, files are hosted in "the cloud" where anyone you want can access them easily; no more clunky intermediaries. The concept of the cloud can be mystifying to people, but

Dropbox has created an interface that is wonderfully intuitive; it gets out of the way and lets users easily see all the files in their "box" without even having to ask, and they don't have to do any file management. Still other such innovative products make tasks like searching, reading, communicating, and buying things easier all the time.

The success you may achieve by finding a new way to remove some hassle shared by the mass public can be staggering. PayPal took away the hassle and danger of exchanging money online, not only for merchants but for all individuals. Netflix has delighted users by removing many hassles, starting with the need to go to a video store at all and the huge annoyance of late fees. More recently it solved the need to remember which episode of a series you watched last by always taking you to the next one when you return to watching that show, no matter how many weeks or months have passed.

NEVER INTRODUCE AN INNOVATION JUST BECAUSE YOU CAN

President Bill Clinton famously said he had engaged in the dalliance with Monica Lewinsky that led to his impeachment for the worst reason to do anything: because he could.

Some products and companies succeed in their innovations because innovation is intrinsic to the value they're offering; it's baked into their very being that they make use of some new technology. Foursquare is a case in point, breaking out by making GPS location the distinguishing feature of its service. But it's easy to rely too much on the value of introducing a cool new technology or feature, and being first to market or in the first wave doesn't always pay off.

As reported by *Business Insider*, car designer Ferdinand Porsche came up with the idea of a hybrid vehicle way back in 1898: the Lohner-Porsche Mixte-Hybrid, which he created for the Lohner Coach company. The batteries it required weighed more than a whole Prius of today, and needless to say, the car failed to take off.[1] One of the most notorious failures of the late-nineties dot-com craze was the home grocery delivery service Webvan. The app Color infamously surfaced and tanked due to its heady but maybe too hip approach to location-based chatting. People just weren't ready to jump into proximity-based chat rooms with strangers.

Technology definitely helps show the way toward innovation, but as influential industrial designer Dieter Rams says, good innovation must always be introduced in tandem with good design, and the key to good design in web products, as we know, is keeping in mind the LEMErS. If the innovation isn't easily learned, efficient, memorable, relatively error-free, and satisfying to users, seriously think about tabling it. Just consider the advantage Steve Jobs achieved by waiting seven years after the release of the first device dubbed a smartphone (the Ericsson R380, put out in 2000 by Ericsson Mobile Communications) to come out with the iPhone. Always watch out for innovation for innovation's sake.

BUSINESS GOALS WILL OFTEN OVERSHADOW UX INNOVATION

Companies and products that boom out of the gate by offering some great innovation for users often run into difficulties in balancing the needs of the business, which may encroach on the beautiful new user experience. Venmo, the former competitor and now subsidiary to PayPal, came onto the scene with a great innovation for users: send money to others for free. Venmo could offer the service for free at first because its business goal at the time, like that of any young startup, was to grow its user base. The goals of the user and that of the business were one and the same. I loved the service, because I could send money to friends with my credit card or pay my rent, all with no surcharge, whereas PayPal takes a fee out of whatever amount of money is being transferred. But once Venmo had grown a large user base, the business goal became to make money and to leverage that user base to do so. The app began charging users a transaction fee. Things presumably worked out well for the founders, because they sold the company to PayPal, but many companies have struggled mightily to make this transition. A key rule here is that the more business goals diverge from user goals, the more care needs to be put into designing the parts of an experience that serve only the business. They must be made as consonant with the positive experience your product offers users as possible.

For a successful example, let's look at how Facebook has evolved. At its start Facebook provided value to its users simply by connecting them to one another. The interface was extremely simple, basically mimicking a phone directory, because that's all that was needed. Too much more might have detracted from the primary goal of its users—to easily get in touch with their friends—and Facebook smartly stayed out of the way. But as the company sought to grow beyond its original user base of college students, it began to innovate more features. Mark Zuckerberg wanted to bring more and more people into the network and to make communicating through it continuously more engaging. Facebook did this by introducing instant messaging, photo storage and tagging, and timelines of events in a user's life. These changes weren't particularly difficult UX challenges, because they were still rooted in the goal of growing the user base and the interface was still not imposing anything unrelated to connecting people. Some users objected to the introduction of the timeline, because it revealed so much all of a sudden about what they'd been up to. Facebook's approach of surprising users with new features has been periodically jarring and has led to many hiccups for the company (about which more later). But ultimately most users became convinced of the benefits of the timeline, or at least habituated to it, because it did in fact serve the user goal of being more closely connected with one's friends. In order to become a viable business in the long term, though, Facebook eventually had to find a way to make revenue, and to do that, like Venmo, they had to leverage the human capital they had built up.

The product teams were charged with creating an experience to sell things like stickers for messaging, ads for brands that kept users on the Facebook platform, and ways of promoting your posts by paying a fee. These were informed product innovations because they were still about enhancing users' interactions with their social network. But they presented real UX challenges. They had to inspire users to interact with things other than their friends' posts and messages while preserving the feelings of personal connection, intimacy, and friendship the site had always offered. When Facebook introduced advertising, the UX demands became even more challenging. The company worked hard to contain the frequency with which users would see ads, as well as to incentivize companies to make their business pages and their ads engaging. Despite much prediction that they would chase their users away, users seem to have accepted this transition as well. Facebook has reportedly not lost significant numbers of users and meanwhile has proven that it is not only a viable business but a booming one. In 2013, the company earned $7.87 billion, and $6.95 billion of that was from advertising revenue.[2]

One of the most important ways in which UX designers can help with this balancing of user and business goals is by finding ways for the features introduced primarily for business purposes to stay out of the way as much as possible. A good example of this is the way the *New York Times* designed its site to enforce its ten-article-per-month limit for nonsubscribers. Once you read five articles, a module docked to the bottom of the screen tells you the count, then again at nine and ten articles, and it's only at that point that you receive a roadblock asking you to subscribe. The timing of presenting the docked module and the roadblock speak to the care that went into aligning the user goals with the business goals. Users are given a good value for free but are also made aware of how much more value a subscription would get them.

One of the real masters of balancing user and business goals in introducing innovations is Google. Consider how the company has innovated with Google Maps. It's continued to offer great user enhancements, such as allowing you to sync the desktop site with the app on your smartphone, which means that your search history gets shared between the devices. So when you look up the address of a restaurant on your desktop at home, that same map will pop up as soon as you check your Google Maps app on your phone when you're getting close to the restaurant. This is incredibly helpful to the user, but it also contributes to Google's business goals in two ways: it builds an ever stronger bond with users, and its incredible utility has allowed the company to begin selling relatively unobtrusive ads at the bottom of the screen without user revolt. This is a great case of innovation being used to serve user and business goals equally.

The value of the service being provided in each of these cases is so apparent to users that they don't fault the product for its need to also serve its business interests. One of the most important rules for introducing innovations is that when users' goals are central to the business goals, innovations should be subtle, almost trying to get out of the way.

One of my favorite innovations that a web product introduced to my life comes from Blue Apron, which provides a subscription service to recipes. It preselects recipes and arranges for delivery of the necessary groceries right to your doorstep. The innovation here is literally invisible. After my initial sign-up where I chose either vegetarian or meat-eater, I've never had to visit the company's website, and it has no app. The only time I interact with the company is through a weekly email telling me what to expect in my delivery, and then in receiving the delivery itself. The best part of this innovation is how small a part Blue Apron plays in the picture.

A SMALLER USER BASE TENDS TO MAKE INNOVATION EASIER

When I think of great UX, many of the examples that come to mind are of sites or apps with relatively small, specialized user bases. This is because a smaller audience tends to mean your users will have more aligned interests in your product, so you have fewer personas to design for. And when you don't need to design for such a large swath of the population, there are fewer ways usability can be influenced. Most often, your users will be familiar with the same set of interactions. If they're older users, say for an AARP app, then touch interactions will be relatively new to them, and they might not like gamification elements; if they're twentysomething gamers, they'll totally expect touch interactions, and they'll find gamification elements appealing (or, beware, they'll have criticisms about how they're done).

Uber, the taxi hailing app, is one product of this kind that has great UX. It has a decent-sized user base, but the company doesn't have to push for huge scale; the product is targeting users of a certain income class in urban areas. It's sustainable for Uber to only ever appeal to this niche, so its decisions about innovations to introduce don't have to take account of other demographics.

Now take the case of Twitter, which is seeking to expand even past its already very large user base. The company has found that some people who go to the site find it hard to grasp how to send tweets, and it wants to bring more users in and get them to interact with tweets more. So it's added a new set of selections at the bottom of every tweet the user is reading for retweeting, quoting a tweet, and other options like emailing a tweet and copying a link to a tweet. Now, this increase of interaction design might be considered bad UX by some. Just how much dumbing down of a product a design should do to appeal to additional users has become a fairly lively topic of discussion among my colleagues. Twitter is sacrificing the minimalist component of great UX for features that help engage less-active users. An alternative approach might be to allow users to customize their interface whichever way they prefer through a settings option. But some would argue that if you don't choose one UX for all users, you are acknowledging that you don't know which is the right answer. Whoever said UX was easy?

I've learned to be okay with criticism about not limiting to one best option. But what I am not okay with is failing to have the right options for current power users and for creating new power users.

POWER USERS ARE YOUR MAVENS

In his influential bestseller *The Tipping Point*, Malcolm Gladwell wrote about the "mavens" who are always trying new products out and then raving about those they love. They're the catalysts of the most powerful means of advertising, word of mouth. On the web, power users are our mavens. These are people who are always quickly learning the newest interfaces, commands, and gestures; they want more out of their product and they max out the efficiencies and enhancing features it offers them, like keyboard shortcuts, gestural commands in touch devices, or simply some options to configure an interface to the power user's preference. You never want to leave them behind. Facilitating power users is definitely the marker of great UX. It means that the product offers a level of usability above the base and lets users take more control of their experience.

The goals of creating a great experience for power users and scaling up do not have to be considered mutually exclusive by any means. One company that's winning at both scale and a great experience is Seamless, the food ordering and delivery service. The largest value they offer is standardizing the UX of restaurant delivery, which sets them up well for going larger scale. But they also offer great options for power users, such as a feature that lets you reorder meals you've previously ordered. This is a simple shortcut to offer that's also unobtrusive to those who don't want to use it, and in effect it creates power users.

Efforts to create power users are easy to make mistakes with; you've got to be sure to keep your eye on the ball of the largest base of users. The first step of being free to focus on appealing to power users is creating consistency in the product that makes it enjoyable for everyone; that then becomes the base for building in shortcuts and special options. And in creating those, you don't have to reinvent the wheel; consider the UX of other products. Lots of shortcuts are common across products; they're like design patterns for power users.

SOMETIMES IT'S BETTER TO ASK FORGIVENESS THAN PERMISSION

When I worked at the *Wall Street Journal*, my designs typically exceeded what development had time for, given the constant performance enhancements and near-annual updates to the operating system that took up so much development time. Months would pass before we'd make polishes or enhancements to a product that had launched, and there was no room for iteration before launch. This is not an uncommon situation in web product development. So one last useful tip about innovating is that when you can't design new features to the highest UX level of efficiency and elegance, but you think they're crucial to add, sometimes you should go ahead with clunkier versions as a start.

I mentioned in the last chapter the *Journal* editor who took it upon himself to add explanatory phrases like "Tap for story" and "Swipe for more," which can still be seen in the video app today. I gave him a hard time for this, but the editor saw it as a necessary Band-Aid to the time it would take to craft a better solution, which wasn't an option given the time constraints on the development team. With a mandate to engage users more and increase article views and with no development time to play with, the editor took the decision into his own hands.

The decision about when to use the "ask forgiveness, not permission" policy is a tricky one. For one thing, you don't want to introduce Band-Aids that become permanent fixtures. You also don't want to teach your users bad habits. In the case of those instructions overlaid on the WSJ Live app, they may have had the side effect of creating dependency, with users coming to rely on them and then pushing back when the more elegant textless versions were introduced. But I've seen time and again how this can be a good way to go ahead and get some innovation done. In fact, it can be a way to keep up with innovation even if your business isn't acknowledging the need for it.

One of the most important skills for a UX designer to cultivate is knowing when to compromise on innovation and be willing to throw some things away, at least for a while. You should never forget to check what the interface guidelines recommend, as they are written in part with this issue in mind. But for the most part, the best way to make the judgment call is with user testing.

DON'T GUESS, TEST

User tests are nothing to be feared. They come in so many varieties that anyone can find a way to work some form of testing into the UX process, even if there's no budget and very little time. User testing is so central to the mission of UX that I'd be moved to say that any design that does not make use of field research is in fact not UX design. Testing is not only the mainstay of understanding how happily users engage with the story you've designed for them and whether they find it easy to follow; it's also vital for surfacing any problems with innovations you're introducing. In my experience, you almost always discover user hopes and expectations you didn't think of, such as a way to go to a particular page you haven't built in. You've got to see people actually using your design in some form of moving prototype to see what they're trying to do with it versus what you've planned for them to do. Most potential users won't be able to articulate the issues to you in interviews. Getting out of my seat with a working prototype that will allow me to test assumptions I'm making about user behavior has always proven a good use of time.

Sometimes user tests can be hugely satisfying. One project I recently worked on had an advanced interaction I had come up with that I really liked but didn't want to get my hopes up about before testing. The project was for a native mobile app that had a mostly image-based content feed. After a whiteboard session where my team and I talked about the contexts, emotions, and behaviors associated with the content, we decided that lots of sharing and conversing would be our core use case. One of the ideas I've wanted to get across in products is that gestures should be a fundamental part of interaction.

Here I decided to introduce a new gesture. It would use the same idea that was behind pull-to-refresh: a second unknown interaction is discovered through the primary interaction. In this case the gesture was swiping vertically through a list. Because a user's swipe is almost never a perfect vertical swipe, a small amount of horizontal movement occurs. I wanted to see if I could somehow use the excess horizontal information received and typically ignored by the system to produce a moment of discovery through unexpected feedback.

I had not yet seen the particular gesture interaction I was thinking of in an app, so I had to make a motion prototype of what it would look like. I used the Hype tool from Tumult for this. This tool allows you to make customized animations, which is extremely useful for testing innovations in interface design, unlike other tools that use built-in animations. After about three hours the animation was done. I showed my developer, and within another day we had a functional prototype. From there I performed what's known as a hallway usability test. Essentially I accosted my coworkers and asked them to swipe through our new feed and check out the design, intentionally not mentioning the gesture interaction.

Each and every person found the interaction unsolicited, meaning it was discoverable. The test was a huge success, and my developer and I were ecstatic. Of course, all we had to do from there was move on to clear the hurdles of visual designs, stakeholder reviews, more user testing, and performance tweaks. No big deal.

I love the process of designing UX innovations of my own and then testing them. I especially like that it's a scientific process, which means you've got to be open to the possibility that your innovation will fail to delight, or might even be missed altogether, and open to changing or abandoning it. Tests allow you to gather hard, empirical evidence, which can be used to defend a design decision or can help you see early enough that you've got to change your plan. You've got to think of the interactive prototypes you're building as the means for testing a hypothesis, not for proving it, and as with all scientific experiments, you have to be careful not to introduce any experimenter bias. The information you collect will help you confirm or revise your understanding of your user personas, will validate or disprove assumptions you've made about how well your design is crafted, and will almost always inspire some good new ideas. You should think of yourself as an anthropologist going out in the field to observe.

My determination to make sure the products I work on are sensitive to users is always fueled by observing people "in the wild" using their mobile devices. I'm continually astonished by the lengths to which people are willing to go to read minuscule type or work their way through a clunky interface. If you catch me in the subway looking over your shoulder at your phone, I'm probably watching how you navigate rather than trying to follow along with the story. I encourage you to always be doing these "field studies." They have been a great source of insight for me, usually showing me what not to do but also helping me think of features I can offer and situations I should try to replicate in user tests.

For apps for mobile devices, if users have told me they are always on the device on the subway, I've conducted tests with subjects standing to see if I can get them to use a device one-handed, because people often have to stand on the subway and hold onto a strap or pole while riding. To test the *Times*' free article-counter feature, I might give users thirty minutes to read several articles and then ask them to tell me about the day's news. This would be a way to simulate their normal reading scenario. It's all about getting as close as possible to actual circumstances, both mentally and physically, for more reliable results. A user tapping a stationary phone on a table or clicking with a mouse when she is accustomed to a trackpad does not represent actual conditions well enough.

TEST OFTEN, TEST EARLY

In influential books about UX by Donald Norman, Steve Krug, and Bill Buxton, the mandate to get your product in front of a user throughout the stages of design and development is at the core. Testing can be done at all stages, from sketches through wireframes, visual mocks, interactive prototypes, and the beta build, and it doesn't stop there. You will also test after product launch. It's always a great surprise to see your product in users' hands. The information gathered in this ongoing user research must not be viewed as secondary to the design process; that's sure to lead to poor user experiences.

Lots of my students, who will surely go on to create more interesting and compelling experiences than I, have objected when I tell them to test a design they're working on, saying that it's not ready to be tested. To this I respond, "It has always been ready."

I often begin testing with a flat wireframe, which is a mock or a wire with semi-intelligent dummy content. It's quick and you can get lots of answers fast. Note that it's important that the users you test at this stage are not on your team. It's tempting to use team members because they're so handy, but they are probably more tech-savvy than most of your users and may also be biased in your favor. The further built out the product is, the less you need to worry about this bias problem, because with a working prototype any glitches become clear to all. When the time comes for you to test a design, you've just got to take a deep breath, acknowledge that it can always be better, and get to it.

At the basic level, a user test is as simple as presenting someone with a static mock and asking them what they think, how they would navigate around it, or what they would want to do from there. Even sketches can be tested, but I suggest doing this with the paper prototypes I described in the last chapter. They're great not only for thinking through your design, but for testing and tweaking things like copywriting, interface icons, and layout.

At their most complex, tests can involve fully functional products with prescreened participants performing tasks and keeping a diary to report on their experiences in using the product for several days. It's not often, though, that UX designers are able to do such elaborate testing, due to time and budget constraints. So learning a few more quick and dirty ways of testing is key.

Before diving into the hows and whens of the kinds of tests I've found most helpful, though, let me give a brief summary of the kinds of tests that have been developed. Over time you may want to learn how to do some or all of these.

The most common user test is an A/B test, in which two designs are compared, either by showing both of them to one group of subjects or by showing one of them to a first group and the other to a second group.

Card sorting is another popular type of test, and is helpful in crafting your information architecture. Users are given a set of words on cards, or the opportunity to make up their own, that are related to a given category of content, such as television shows. They're asked to rank or group the cards according to preference, which helps you understand the best labeling and ordering for your content. I used this method recently to gauge user preferences for having a list of names of particular television programs over first choosing from genres, such as sports and comedy. In the exercise I used a closed set of twenty TV stations, shows, and genres of various depth, such as sports versus football versus NFL.

Data collection through online analytics is a way of testing a large number of live users. This is done by using plug-and-play services like Google Analytics or Chartbeat to monitor activity over time or, in the case of the latter, in real time. You see where users are most active, which features they're ignoring, what parts of the day they're visiting, which ads are getting clicks, and much more.

Remote testing with tools like Silverback, Usability.com, or Userfeel .com is a way of conducting task analysis and scenario-based testing from afar. In these types of tests users are given a specific task, like composing and sending an email. The tester then observes the user's efforts through recorded video, a screen-sharing program, or maybe over a video phone service like Skype. In one form of a remote test, the "think aloud" method, you ask the user to describe what she's doing and report on the experience as she goes. This method can also be used for person-to-person tests. The distance helps make sure you're not giving the user any hints or leading pointers about how to do the task. It also allows you to test more users relatively inexpensively and from a wide range of locations; you can see how people in urban areas use your product differently from those in smaller towns, for example. For remote tests, I've found the hardest part is getting users to talk about their thought process, so careful examination of their interactions, instincts, and emotions is absolutely necessary.

A long-established type of user test is focus groups, but I advise against these because a good amount of research has shown that they are ineffective in getting reliable user feedback. This is for complicated reasons, among them that the situation is so removed from real life that members of the group tend to influence one another's answers, and that for whatever reasons, people often misrepresent their true behavior or feelings about a product idea or prototype in this setting.

TESTING IN THE REAL WORLD

Data analytics and remote testing programs are making those kinds of testing cheaper and easier to do all the time. But as I've said, most often the budget of both time and money for testing is very limited, and it's common that no formal testing will be prescribed for you to do until a full prototype is created—if then. So I encourage you not to wait for testing to be requested. I know in my career I've always had to go above and beyond what the job description called for, and one thing that has meant is conducting usability tests of my own, through any means possible, and I know the same is true for lots of UX designers. When people ask me what I test with, the answer is whatever I can get my hands on.

Testing a full working prototype before launch is always advised. Just think of the debacle of the Obama administration's launch of the HealthCare.gov site any time you're tempted to forgo the process. Nothing else will reveal problems in a product the way giving users an actual working version does. As a UX designer, you won't be in charge of ordering such tests. But as I discussed in the previous chapter, less polished forms of prototypes have become easy to make, and you can make them yourself, no developer required, at even the earliest stages of design.

Before I started working in UX, when I thought of a prototype, I thought of those space-age-looking concept cars that I would never be able to drive, not only because they were one-off experiments that could at times be described as priceless, but also because they weren't street legal or even built with working engines inside. After I got into UX, the concept at first took on the new meaning of a functioning stand-in for the real thing. The thinking was that prototypes needed to be near real to test on subjects, otherwise people might not take tests seriously and engage fully enough with the product. The better I got at prototyping, the more I learned to return to my original way of thinking about them, as hypothetical constructs—as a way of testing the future. Which brings me back to innovation. Prototyping is no longer an expensive luxury; it's actually the cheapest way to find out if something conceptually fantastical is in fact practical.

GRAB PEOPLE IN THE HALLWAY

During my career I have found that most methods need not be very rigorous to be successful. I advise adjusting the types of testing you do to the expediencies you're dealing with and to what seems to work best for you. One colleague of mine believes in a quiet approach, just sitting in a room with a test subject, giving him the product to play with, and not asking questions. By virtue of how awkward it is to be alone in a room with someone else who remains silent, the user breaks the silence by spontaneously offering responses to the product, which prevents the tester from biasing reactions or limiting results to the things she already knows she wants to test. I prefer a more informal type of test, generally called a hallway or guerrilla usability test, in which I chat with users and ask them to perform scenario-based tasks such as searching for an article or searching for and buying an item.

Whichever style you opt for, one rule always applies: be aware of yourself.

I want that to be the first thing you think when going into a usability test. In my user tests I always know when I have gone off script or accidentally used a word that's too leading. Going off script is not necessarily a bad thing; as I said earlier about initial user interviews, it can mean discovering some useful, unexpected things that may help you in the test, such as if the subject mentions she really loves something a competitor product is doing. But if it means talking too much or giving away any clues, then it can lead to a tainted test. It's best to do only 20 percent of the talking, at most, during a user test. You want to hear as much as you can from your subject in the small window you get.

The guerrilla test is my most used type of live user test. Here is how a typical one goes for me. I sit in a well-trafficked area where I know a certain user type will be. In my current job, this is in the break room on the largest floor of our building. I sit at a table with a little sign that says HELP MAKE OUR APPS BETTER and snag passersby as they come and go. I often have to call out "Good afternoon!" to get them to come over. It takes some time to get used to this; engaging with a stranger can be awkward. My wife is a journalist and I don't know how she does it half the time (she says it takes resolve and getting over people saying no). Lots of people turn me down, but eventually some kind soul will give me her time and the test begins.

I like to ask a few introductory questions to get some context about the user and how she is similar to one of my personas or different in a way I haven't thought of in my personas yet. One thing these tests are good for is providing more information with which to refine your personas. You also want to ask users some questions at this point that will fill you in about how familiar and comfortable they are with the kind of features you're testing. For example, I ask people what email client they use on their phones and if they could show me how to delete a piece of spam. Given that most email clients support a gesture-based way of deleting an email from the inbox, this allows me to note which users understand and use gesture controls. Then, if there is a gesture-based control in the product I am testing, I know which subjects are more likely to find that feature. If during the test even the gesture-savvy users don't find the feature, then I've found a significant issue.

My interview questions tend to focus on the activity I'm testing. For example, if I'm testing a video-watching product, I will ask whether the subject currently uses any mobile video apps and if so, what kinds of videos she likes to watch and where she usually watches them, such as at home or on the way to work. These quick questions do wonders to tell you which tasks you should ask which subjects to perform. Depending on the amount of time you have for each test, you can have a more in-depth interview. For the tests I conduct in the break room, I typically don't have enough time for long interviews.

What I'm interested in catching with these small and quick tests are overarching usability issues, typically with interactions, the hierarchy of information, navigation, and labeling or copywriting. To uncover problems, I give the users tasks to complete based on the information gleaned from the short interview. I generally focus on the tasks core to the product. If I'm testing a reading app and my user says she usually scans articles for an important one to read, I would ask him to do just that. Here's a sample of how a test might unfold:

TESTER: Good afternoon! Have a few minutes to help test out this new video app?

SUBJECT: Sure.

TESTER: Before we start, can I ask if you have used this or any other app to watch video on your phone?

SUBJECT: I watch Netflix on the bus sometimes.

TESTER: Oh, great! How do you like it?

SUBJECT: It's good at what it does, which is keep my place in the TV series I'm watching.

TESTER: Oh yeah, that is a nice feature. Okay, let's get started then. I want you to imagine yourself on the bus Monday morning. You've finished your TV series over the weekend and are interested in checking out a new video app you downloaded. Start the app and find a video that is interesting to you.

I always start off in a friendly way, in a warm voice, which can do wonders to put your subject at ease and or get her out of the mindset that she's taking a test. Many UX professionals recommend also stating that it is the product being tested and not the subject and asking subjects to be brutally honest, saying that any negative feedback won't hurt your feelings, in order to elicit uncensored responses, which can be very revealing about any confusion or frustration they're having.

You should always pay close attention not only to what subjects say but to little unspoken revelations, like a look of disgust or a smirk and chuckle—these are as important as any verbal feedback. I always make it a point to ask my subjects what provoked such a reaction, and much useful information comes from that.

I might be criticized for leaving out some statements from my test script above, like asking the subject to think out loud or the point about brutal honesty, but my method is comfortable for me, and it's worked well. As I said, you should feel free to tailor your methods to best suit you.

CLARIFYING YOUR PRIORITIES

The results from these early tests always help me figure out the order of importance of problems to address. You want to give top priority to meeting the expectations and desires of users. The second priority is assessing the success of the design in achieving the business goals. That's right, I said it: business goals come second. But this doesn't mean you don't take them very seriously. You want to use your tests to help figure out how to bring the business goals and user goals into alignment. If the business goals are not aligned with those of the users, such as with the *New York Times* needing to charge a subscription fee when users want free content, then it's important to think of every way you can possibly make achieving the business goals less of a pain.

The *New York Times* came up with the feature that counts the number of free articles users have read per month and then alerts them when they've reached the limit. Just think about how users might react if suddenly they couldn't read any more articles and weren't told why. In addition to showing consideration to users, this might be a great feature for converting free readers to subscribers. If I were still working at the *Wall Street Journal*, I'd be interested in testing a similar feature in comparison with the icon that indicates articles that only subscribers may view. Or say a business goal is appealing to power users. Maybe your product has three flows that accomplish the task of deleting an item, and in your tests you discover only the longest one is being used; you may want to introduce educational features to transition base users into power users.

Testing business goal features such as whether advertising is clicked on or users sign up for newsletters may be harder than testing the user-oriented features, because test subjects may not want to perform them; often they require steps that can be barriers to entry, like entering personal information, linking accounts, or pulling out a credit card. But it is important to probe users for their thoughts on the screens that ask them to complete these actions exactly because of the high friction involved with them.

INTERPRETING USER FEEDBACK

The most recent lesson I have come to learn through the trials of my career is how to interpret user feedback. The most difficult part is realizing that people often don't really know what they want or what they may become just fine with. Lots of Facebook users might have said they wouldn't want ads appearing in their news feeds, but most have adjusted to them readily. Also, sometimes giving users what they want is impossible, whether because of the programming it would involve or because it conflicts with business goals, like removing all advertising.

In a recent project for a mobile application I worked on, a series of user tests exposed an issue with navigation. Users expected to dive right into a category after tapping on the navigation item for it, but tapping actually took them to a scrolling animation that allowed them to move up or down the page to the corresponding point. The navigation wasn't a link to the deeper sections of the product. If I didn't have a close connection to the product I might have advised changing the navigation to do just what the user wants. But I knew that another level of navigation could actually get in the way of how people interacted with the product overall, because they liked to read in all sorts of categories. We should always keep in mind that any additive solution fundamentally changes the flow. A deeper section to the navigation might have led users to lose their place in the app, and that can cause drop-offs in usage. You often want to reshape user expectations rather than react directly to their feedback. This can make the difference between users adapting to a product's innovations and the product adapting to the users, which can often limit innovation.

In the example just mentioned, instead of adding in another page and transition, I redesigned so that when users tap the navigation the scroll highlights the item tapped, making it easier to scroll to it. As interaction design professionals we have a responsibility to discover multiple ways of presenting a solution before resorting to a larger design change.

TESTING THE COMPETITION

Another great testing practice is to do user tests with competitive products. Obviously, if there are features in the competition that you plan to include as well, performing task analyses to find the pros and cons of their implementation and design can save you boatloads of time and money. I've found that examining competitors is a great way to get an idea of where an experience needs performance improvements, polish, or a fundamental overhaul. This is in keeping with an aphorism on innovation from Amazon founder Jeff Bezos that I read in *Fortune* magazine: "Your margin is my opportunity."[3]

First off, I have found it important to become a power user of competitors, or at least to try to explore every part of the competitive products before I begin my designs. This is your first type of competitor testing. Performing user tests of a competitor's product as if it were your own can also reveal things you haven't observed about the product. These tests can also help you focus on what makes you different. In the pretest interviews you should ask whether the subject is a fan of the product and why or why not. Always ask users what they currently do to perform the tasks you are interested in, what they like about the way the product lets them do it, and what the apps would do in a perfect world. Then, ask them to either show or tell you the process step-by-step, depending on if it is real or hypothetical.

Other users can help identify positive features and mistakes that you might not have picked up on. Because I've been working on reading on mobile for some time now, I've been interested in interface innovations that help navigation through content without getting in the way. On one recent project I explored using a touch interface feature that would let users swipe to the next article immediately after they finished one. I'd seen this interaction first in an RSS reader app for iOS named Reeder and again in the CNN app. In order to make the case for its use in the project I was working on, I decided to test the feature's effectiveness. I sought out users of the CNN app, told them I was doing a usability test on it, and asked them to show me around the product. For people who described themselves as daily users I expected to see the swipe-to-next-article feature in action, but when they showed me the app no one made mention of it. They would scroll through the articles for a little bit, skimming the text, stopping maybe to look at a video because that is what CNN is more known for, but always tapping back to the list of articles before picking another one. After three tests no one was actually scrolling to the bottom to even discover the swipe-to-next-article feature. Puzzled, I wondered if my test methods were somehow wrong.

I changed the test to include time for reading. Instead of having users show me around, I asked them to give me a brief summary of three articles and to take as much time as they needed. As I observed their interactions I saw that my next user dutifully read through the text and arrived at the bottom only to just miss the feature. But the test let me discover there was a very good reason for this—the feature was buggy. Near its last iteration in the CNN iOS app version 1.95 (build 4263) the "loop" feature, as it's described in the Tips & Tricks section of the app, does not display the first time a user swipes past the bottom of the article and the feature was abandoned altogether as of the latest version, 2.20 (build 4917).

MINING THE DATA

In testing, you want to go both micro and macro. A few face-to-face hallway usability tests can help you be sensitive to individual differences in preferences and experience. But to determine what issues are affecting the largest number of your users, you'll need to do some data mining.

One of the most accessible, and potent, sources of user data is reviews in the Apple App Store or the Android Marketplace. But rather than just reading through them, as instructive (and bone chilling) as this can be, you want to do some analysis of them. The Apple App Store allows you to export all user reviews (or a subset) to your computer so you can search through them in all sorts of ways. I've also taken the tedious route of copying and pasting available user feedback from other platforms. In analyzing these comments, I've found it instructive to group them into general buckets by issue addressed, such as system performance; data quality; and subcategories of UX issues, like navigation, layout and information architecture, and feature requests. I suggest you try bucketing by writing them out on sticky notes and then grouping together ones that fall under broad categories, such as feature requests or app crashes. This helps you focus on which issues to prioritize.

Unfortunately this technique isn't relevant for websites, because there are no gateways with public consumer feedback for websites as there are for apps. The closest thing might be a search results page where user feedback is evidenced in the rank of the site on the page, but that doesn't provide you the glaring comments you get in reviews. Every once in a while there is a kind soul who cordially explains her wants and dislikes in an email. For the most part, though, you've got to go to the analytics programs.

Analytics and tracking tools tell you where users come from; how long they stay on a certain page; or how often they use different features like logging in, sharing, or completing any other task. Depending on the platform, some tools, like crash reports for native apps, are built in. With websites you need active participation from the team to build in analytics tools to capture user session data.

Teasing useful insights for UX out of this data is a craft more than a science at this point. The data you collect concerning time spent on a page might point toward more and less successful elements of the interaction design. You might trace user drop-offs to database call failures. Or patterns in where users are spending the most time might point to some content that is especially effective. These tools are still emerging and are sure to become ever more sophisticated. Some of the newest tools I've seen for collecting and analyzing mobile product usage capture gestures of users and then display information about the gestures during sessions visualized on top of each view. This allows you to literally watch for errors or trends of usage by finger movement. The kicker is when you get to string these recorded sessions together to watch an individual user over time. You can see a user routine set in, and that's a great way to evaluate learnability and memorability.

RELEASE, FIX, RELEASE

There is one last type of testing to discuss. The kinds of user tests I've covered are the next best thing you can do to actually shipping the product, and some leading web companies have famously made a practice of going ahead and doing testing by shipping, releasing their products to the wild. Shipping products has become an audacious form of prototyping.

Facebook has been one big advocate of this, and you could say the company is in a state of perpetual prototyping. According to the *Mashable* article "Facebook Launches Redesigned Mobile App for iOS 7," the company did six months of testing leading up to the final release of its iOS7 redesign, in which "1 to 2 million users [were] unknowingly utilizing versions of the redesigned navigation bar."[4] Such a large test is known as a bucket test. Fully functional versions of an app or feature are tested on the broad public. Google also has a long history of publicly testing new products in beta versions. Gmail was one such innovation, and it was in beta for five years, being tested and updated until the beta label was removed in 2009 after developers integrated security improvements, document viewing, increased storage space, and a mobile-optimized version.

This may be the best way to get lots and lots of user feedback fast, and it can be viewed as an especially careful way of going about innovation because it allows for testing with so many users. But it also clearly has its dangers, prime among them being that it often means failing publicly. The UX leaves a lot to be desired, and many products from both of these companies have had less than celebratory receptions at release. Many innovative startups have also espoused a "Fuck it, ship it" approach, opting to constantly update their products, with no one version ever being considered final. These ways of operating are based on a credo of "failing fast," getting actual products out there and then quickly updating them. The companies that advocate this way of operating, and its public failure, can do so in part because they have big development teams, which means they can fix fast as well. For most companies, failing privately, testing on smaller groups of users, is the way to go. Steve Krug has argued that testing with just three to five real users will catch 80 percent of usability issues. I know I've found that my quick and dirty hallway tests have been invaluable, and most often this smaller-scale testing that you initiate on your own is going to be your best means of getting real user feedback all the way through your design process.

Knowing when and how to innovate is a hallmark of good UX

practice. You should always strive to move products forward and to bring your users along on that path to the future. But you've also got to get used to leaving lots of your ideas on the cutting room floor. Test early and test often, arm yourself with the best user data and analytics you can, and always be prepared to put an innovation on hold. Chances are good you'll be able to come back to it, and with the rate of evolution of digital products, you may not have to wait long.

POINTS TO REMEMBER

Innovation Is Not for Innovation's Sake

» You are a key player in helping users make their way on the path to the future; always be considering how you can make good use of an innovative interaction or systems capability.

» Also keep in mind, though, that introducing innovations to users can be treacherous and that innovations must clearly serve users' needs, not your desire to introduce them.

» The best innovations take work away from users.

» Innovations must also serve the business goals, and your ability to introduce them will often be driven by business mandates. One of the most important roles of UX design is to balance user and business goals in innovation.

» Always consider your power users; they will be the most eager adopters of innovations and will be hungry for them. But you must find ways to please them without alienating less tech-savvy users.

» User tests don't need to be formal and elaborate; quick hallway tests can provide you with a great deal of insight, and you can conduct them all through the design and building process.

(continued)

- When you can, conduct tests to simulate as closely as possible the context in which users will be making use of the product.
- Testing with competitors' products can provide great insight into new features to offer and those to avoid.
- Make good use of hard data. Gather all the data you can by making use of every tool from site analytics to user reviews.

Chapter 5

GOOD UX COMES FROM BEING OPEN TO INPUT

One of the things I like best about being a UX designer is the community of people I get to work with and the creativity they bring to our work. On every project I am sure to encounter new obstacles and also make new discoveries, and it's been eye-opening to learn how many members of the team have a hand in helping me craft and find solutions. I may have the chance to work with the developers on a cool new interface or design pattern, or to learn about a new subject from the content team, as I've done with news and media at Yahoo in working on the different apps we put out. Particularly with the Yahoo Finance app, the differences between how Yahoo and the *Wall Street Journal* work have been illuminating about how good UX comes from the whole team. At the *Journal* we had a huge editorial team that created the content and ultimately shaped the experience. At Yahoo, we have a much smaller editorial staff and much of the content we serve is from other sites across the web. But what Yahoo lacks in editorial staff, it more than makes up for in development talent. The developers at Yahoo are less educated about the nuances of what makes a great finance news story, but that doesn't stop them from understanding how to engineer tools to compensate. The search and analysis algorithms they've written and the powerful personalization engine they've built allow us to create an experience that stands up to that of the *Journal* app. I couldn't begin to write those algorithms, but I do know about the requirements for a sophisticated personalization engine for content delivery. It takes all of us to make something great.

I love interacting with my team on projects. I would say that about half of my time is spent in collaboration: going over sketches, working on layouts, exploring animations, finessing interactions, and learning from the developers how we can make great use of new technology. The designers and developers I've been able to work with have never ceased to amaze me with their command of their crafts and the ways they can take an idea of mine and push it to do something so much better than I could ever have thought of. With one idea of mine for a project I'm still working on, I wanted to replicate in an app the experience of going to one of those photo booths in which you can get a whole strip of photos of yourself taken. When I showed my rough design to a colleague, he noted that I was using a number of different screens for taking the photos and then sharing or printing them, which was more complicated than the way the photo booths work. "Think of it," he said. "When you sit in a real photo booth all you have to do is put in your money, wait for the flashes, make some funny faces, and bam, the photos come out. It's all done in two places: in front of the camera and next to the booth waiting for your photos." I took another stab at the interface and boiled it down to just two screens, one for inside the booth and one for outside. From such a spur-of-the-moment interchange, I was able to create a much more elegant and evocative design.

The creativity of UX work was what drew me to it in the first place, and doing the job has taught me a whole lot about creativity. I've learned, for one, that there are a number of popular myths about the creative process, and that appreciating the truths behind those myths is an enormous benefit in doing UX work. One of the most misguided of those is that the best ideas spring forth out of people's brains solely through the magical workings of some special creativity neurons. Creativity tends to be thought of as a solo pursuit. But I've come to appreciate how much creativity can come out of collaboration, and how you never know where and from whom good ideas will come. The poet John Donne famously wrote, "No man is an island / Entire of itself / Every man is a piece of the continent / A part of the main."[1] The same must be said for the UX designer.

It's important to see UX not as just the UX designer's work, but as a collaborative process. Not only are users essential partners, but so are the rest of the product team and the stakeholders, and understanding how to be an open-minded, collaborative member of the product team is essential. This makes the process of incorporating UX into projects work smoothly, but the input of team members can lead you to some great new ideas and save you from pitfalls.

I had a fantastic experience recently collaborating on a feature of the new finance app for Yahoo. The company had brought in an absolutely brilliant student, Jonathan Willing, as an intern. He's a real bad-ass tech whiz, and they had him working on front-end development. We implemented an animation technology he developed that makes use of what's called spring physics, which allows you to design iOS animations with a whole set of highly refined parameters for properties such as momentum, dampening, and acceleration. (He's made the code open source, and it's available at https://github.com/jwilling/JNWSpringAnimation.)

The resulting animations are truly visually striking, and I worked with Jon to animate a loading indicator for the app, which, in my humble opinion, looks great and has been very well received. I would never have been able to ask my full-time front-end people to do something like that for our first version of the app, because it was viewed as a flourish that wasn't core to the app, and I would never have known about the technology if I weren't keeping my ears open and willing to learn from Jon.

The development of digital products is one of the most dynamic and creative endeavors of our time, and it attracts incredibly talented people who come to it from all sorts of educational backgrounds and prior work experience. I've been able to collaborate with designers who work exclusively in the motion graphics tool After Effects, making sure every element they put on the screen has life and personality. They've taught me a great deal about just how dynamic graphics can be. A web developer I worked with at the *Wall Street Journal* ran a game development studio on the side that pushed the limits of the hardware a web browser can access on a smartphone. He taught me how to harness the accelerometer to make an app's display shift perspective with the user's movements. You absolutely want to tap into the experience of your coworkers. And hey, you never know who's going to be the next Loren Brichter or Amanda Cox who might bring you along in a breakout new avenue, or with what brilliant colleague you may be able to create your own experience.

YOU'RE NOT THE OWNER OF THE UX

In order to benefit optimally from collaboration, it's important that you not think of UX design as a narrow, siloed skill set, or of yourself as being in a "UX bubble." Even if you are a dedicated, specialist UX designer, you've got to be constantly interacting with the other members of the product team, sharing ideas, getting feedback, and solving problems. You shouldn't think of yourself as "owning" the UX, because you want everyone on the team to feel dedicated to it and to appreciate what UX has to offer. You're also not ever going to be the only one tasked with UX input. Gathering user data, for example, is not only the job of UX, but is usually done by the marketing people and the product manager as well. Even specialized engineers are involved in collecting usage data that can point toward trends in how and when a product is being used. You want to be able to tap into their data, and you want them to make use of yours.

Being open when helping others on the team will greatly enhance your ability to shape good ideas and feedback. Over time, being collaborative can encourage others on the team to think of ways to contribute to your efforts, as well as make them more receptive to your ideas and appreciative of the value of UX. Empathy is important not only in regard to users, but also to all those you're working with to make the product. The better a team member you are, the more effective you will be and the more you'll find that your own creativity and problem solving are enhanced. So first in this chapter I want to discuss some of the ins and outs of collaborating with the team. Then I'll discuss how a receptivity to outside input goes way beyond working with your team and testing with users. Sometimes the best UX ideas will come from entirely unexpected sources.

PLAYING WELL WITH OTHERS

There's no question that the process of collaboration can be challenging. For one thing, when the interests of users and those of the business clash, which is just about inevitable on many projects, someone has to compromise. That can be hard. I've seen more parts of my designs hit the cutting room floor than I'd care to recall, and I still wish I could get a do-over on some of those. It can seem as if product managers and the higher-ups making decisions on what to cut and what to move forward with always want to take the easiest path to completion, and the least expensive. This used to bother me much more than it does now. Learning to empathize with the pressure those decision-makers are under and how hard it is to decide where to allocate limited resources has helped me get over this hurdle.

The most common question I get in my classes is, "How do you deal with team members and stakeholders who don't care about UX?" My answer is listen to them, even when they won't listen to you. This is the advice I got from the head of UX at the *Wall Street Journal*, who told me she often had a hard time with this issue herself. She taught me to see that if you understand where they are coming from, you can redirect your energies more readily to figuring out how to do your best work within your limits.

Don't get me wrong. The degree to which others on the team may not appreciate or understand the role of UX, how UX research works, and how it can improve products can really be frustrating. Never assume people have the same understanding of UX that you do or that they believe in its methods. It's often hard to get colleagues to appreciate how much research goes into UX; lots of people think of UX as primarily about sitting at the computer making things pretty.

A friend of mine who's a UX designer was just venting to me about how her product manager told her that he didn't want her to do user tests from wireframes, he wanted her to do her first tests with a higher-fidelity prototype. She knew that meant she'd probably waste time making the prototype because problems that would otherwise come up in testing from the wires wouldn't be caught, and she'd probably have to do an additional prototype test thereafter. He wasn't having any of it, and she had no choice but to do it his way.

One key problem is that the different members of a development team tend to privilege their own components of the project, and that can lead to some real struggles. Visual designers will sometimes push for a beautiful design that is just not serving the user or business needs well enough; a design can be beautiful but distracting or off message. Front-end developers can succumb to feature creep because they've fallen in love with some new interaction that may not be of any interest to your audience. You may have to pull them back, sometimes kicking and screaming, from "enhancing" a product with things most users won't ever notice. And back-end engineers will sometimes object to your ideas before you've even been able to describe them, because they see them as requiring too much programming. But, after all, UX designers tend to privilege their own chief concerns, too. I'd venture to guess that most of us would be pretty happy if no site or app had to feature standardized space advertising, not only because it is so easy to dismiss for the user, but because so often ads intrude on the experiences you can shape. But, of course, this is just not the way the business works sometimes.

I started this book off by pointing out that users have a very wide range of familiarity and comfort with technology. Well, those on development teams have a very wide range of familiarity and appreciation of UX. The Lean UX method, which I'll introduce later in this chapter, was developed largely because so many teams doing Agile software development, which stresses speed of process, didn't want to make time for doing UX research, especially for creating key deliverables of UX design like personas and wireframes. The developers of Lean UX found a way to incorporate some key concepts and methods from UX, like sketches and prototypes, into a new overall development process. This highlights another lesson I've learned about UX: it's not a lockstep process that always has to be done in one way, and parts of the basic process can be dispensed with as time, management support, and the experience of those on the team call for.

Even if you are a dedicated UX designer like me, you're never going to be able to do all the user research you'd really like to or convince your product manager and development team of everything you'd like to do with a design. But the more you learn to work with the entire team, speak the language of each of their specialties, and account for their concerns and issues, the more you're going to get support for your ideas and create what you'd like to see.

The team members a UX designer works the most closely with are the visual designer, the front-end developer, and the product manager, and I've learned some helpful lessons about the pitfalls to look out for with each and how to make your interactions with them as productive and smooth as possible.

AREN'T VISUAL DESIGNERS JUST PIXEL PUSHERS?

If you are a dedicated UXer not in charge of visual production assets, you're always going to work closely with your visual designer. This is one of the crucial roles of UX, but the relationship can be fraught for a number of reasons. For one thing, many visual designers working in the digital space have come from working in print media or advertising, and some have limited understanding of the very different qualities and challenges of the digital canvas. I've found that some don't pay enough attention to the interactions and what users need visually in order to optimize those interactions, such as clear feedback and good copy. For example, they might be pushing for a minimalist look, which has been so popular in recent years, and produce a design with no labels at all on the home page, just icons they think users will know how to discern. But lots of users want clear labels, and icons can be a good deal more ambiguous than designers may think they are. Have you ever driven in a foreign country and encountered road signs with graphics that were a total mystery? Everyone on the planet is going to understand what a kangaroo crossing sign is warning about.

(Courtesy of Peter Firminger)

But what exactly is this supposed to mean?

(Courtesy Shutterstock)

Well, sure, pay attention—but to what? It's used in many countries to alert drivers of some kind of hazard ahead, but what should they be looking out for? This version is from Germany, and in fact it's often accompanied by another sign, which might show a car driving on a rough road or rocks falling from an embankment. That's not a very elegant design solution.

Visual designers also tend not to focus on content, and one reason is they often have to start working before the actual content is ready, so they work with dummy text. A common problem is that they'll make a design with text that looks great but won't be representative of the final product's content. They may also want to break conventions, like those found in human interface guidelines, which can lead to confusion for users.

Much has been made of how Steve Jobs said that Apple didn't design according to customers' desires because customers don't know what they really want until you give it to them. To his point, what user could have told Jonathan Ive, chief of design at Apple, that he wanted the iPhone interface to look and feel the way it does? What do users know about creating a home page as sparse and yet engaging as Google's? I've even read some arguments that the fundamental talents required to be a good UX designer are different from those that make for a talented visual designer; supposedly good UX people are better conceptual thinkers and have a better grasp of psychology, and visual designers are more creative and innovative. This kind of crude generalization is bunk.

Visual designers can definitely be myopic and headstrong about working with a more purely aesthetic set of goals. There are certainly times this can drive you crazy. But I've also found that they can work absolute wonders with what I'm proposing in my sketches and wireframes, and there are so many ways they can help tell the story of a product. Visual designers tend to be marvelous storytellers, understanding how to use color, type, photography, and even white space to convey a clear and powerful message for your company or client. You absolutely want to harness that talent for your users.

I've found that by learning some of their language and how to see through their eyes, I can better appreciate both what designers are aiming for and how to work with them to make sure usability needs are covered. Steve Jobs may have said users don't know what they want until they see it, but he also vigorously insisted that Apple designs have superior usability. I've found that many visual designers deeply understand how vital usability is and have it as a key goal. We can collaborate most effectively when I bring in the cognitive perspective, helping them see how users are going to be thinking when they encounter a design. Visual design really is a language, and it's definitely worth taking the time to become at least basically proficient in it. This will allow you not only to convey to designers that you respect and understand their craft, at least to a degree, but also to brainstorm about ideas with them.

The first design project in my career that I felt was truly my own was for a tablet application for MarketWatch. The designer I was working with, Anna Kardaleva, had just come from HBO and was far more experienced than I was. She taught me so much about the language of visual design and ways to focus a user's attention. She also gave me free rein to make mistakes and learn things on my own. For the many wireframes I came up with she would riff on my ideas, and we'd throw thoughts back and forth. Anna taught me things like the nuances of iconography and how you can use color choice to signal the function of an interaction, such as making all clickable icons purple. She was a branding expert and helped me appreciate how to work with a brand's story. She drew a wealth of different icons and we would take them around to the visual design team to get feedback on which was best for representing the page for mutual fund data or that for industrial stocks. The value of doing such quick spot tests with colleagues was a revelation for me, and as you've seen, it's a technique I've made a standard part of my process.

You can also develop good relationships with visual designers by explaining how changes in technology will impact designs. With designing for touch screens now so important, all of us are learning a new design language, and helping visual designers understand the language of touch and what users are expecting from a touch screen is an important terrain of collaboration. UX specialists and visual designers must work together to create what are being called natural user interfaces (NUIs), as opposed to graphical user interfaces. NUIs are meant to be highly intuitive so that little or no learning is needed for users.

Author and speaker Josh Clark and my friend and web designer Jennifer Brook are great sources of information on this subject. A talk I saw Clark give, called "Buttons Are a Hack," was revolutionary to my education in this area, and I've worked hard to bring its message to my visual design team. The message is that because we no longer have the mouse cursor to act as an intermediary with the display, we lose certain interactions like hover states and scrolling, and new visual cues are often needed to guide users. The clearest example of this is the scroll. In the mouse environment we typically saw an up or down arrow to click on that would make the screen move up or down. With a touch interface, we want instead to create an interaction that feels natural to do with an index finger or thumb, and for scrolling, that is to drag our finger in the direction we want the text to move. But how does visual language signify this available interaction? Clark calls for a new language to solve such problems, and we are beginning to see creative solutions, many of which rub against the grain of the established best practice in web design, which is to have clean, precise pages. We're seeing things like lines of text cut off and even pieces of images peeking out from the edge of the screen, which are harnessing the laws of human visual perception.

The two examples above play on the law of symmetry, discovered in Gestalt psychology, which says that humans have an innate ability to perceive that a whole object exists when only part of it is visible and to perceive that object's center of gravity. When some text or part of a graphic is cut off or an element trails past the visual boundaries of the page, we are naturally inclined to play with the screen to find the rest. We're just in the early phase of crafting the NUI language, and I strongly encourage you to learn all you can about it in order to become a good contributor to the product's visual design.

DEVELOPERS ARE THE MASTERS OF THE MEDIUM

I'll never forget the first time I saw one of the painter Yves Klein's signature monochrome blue works. Klein had played around with the ultramarine blue pigment that's part of every painter's tool kit to enhance the way it would appear on canvas. He learned how to blend it with a synthetic resin that allowed the pigment to retain its vividness of color much better than the traditional resin. The effect was so striking that Klein painted a series of works devoted purely to the color, which is named International Klein Blue, and they went on to become his most famous pieces. If you've never seen one, I encourage you to take any opportunity you may have to do so; the experience is intense.

What's relevant about this for UX is that Klein understood the medium of paint so well, down to the details of its chemical composition, that he was able to do something groundbreaking that was also incredibly simple and basic.

Good developers understand the medium of the digital space so well that they can help you achieve your goals for a product by finding ways to play with the medium. It's awesome to me how some of them can mold and shape a site to fulfill a design I've given them, and often to significantly improve it. In a recent research project I was working on, a developer colleague of mine took a motion prototype I'd given him and brought it to life but gave it properties I hadn't even thought possible, using animation physics similar to the spring physics the Yahoo intern helped me work with. Developers can also be of enormous help in solving performance problems with a design. One of the foundational standards of good code is that faster is better, and developers can work wonders to speed up elements of your design, like interactions and page transitions. Performance is also defined by the quality of the interaction experience, such as whether a scroll down a page feels smooth or jerky.

Front-end engineering that affects UX isn't always so obvious. After I left the *Journal*, an update to the flagship iPad app came out that allowed users to put a URL bookmark on the home screen of the iPad that opened the app. This feature released the app from the clutches of the dreaded Newsstand folder. UX research had shown that sequestering an app icon in a folder greatly reduced the chances of a user opening it, and Apple had done just that by introducing Newsstand for all newspapers and magazines. My former development team had figured out a work-around, and when I saw the new release I cheered them for the achievement. This was a great UX feature that only someone with knowledge of how the system worked could have come up with. Being a master of the medium leads to so many opportunities for crafting an experience.

Front-end developers aren't the only ones who can produce engineering that enhances an experience. Back-end engineers can do a great deal to apprise you of features you can include in a design. Sometimes just exploring systems options is an effective way to generate ideas, and only the handler of the medium the product is built from can comprehend all the options available. Back-end engineers can help you understand what is possible and how it can be implemented.

During my graduate school years at the School of Information and Library Science, the most valuable classes I took were on databases, information systems, and metadata. Metadata in particular was an interesting subject, introducing me to the seemingly endless knowledge that data can have about itself. The things that any digital object can tell you about itself, such as its origin, its location in a database, its size, and the type of object it is—whether an ebook, music video, or photograph—limit the ways in which it can be linked to other digital objects and how it can be searched for. A good example is the metadata for the digital object that represents a book in an online store. If the data doesn't know the object represents a romance novel, that book won't come up in searches for that category. The ability to connect, or link, digital objects may be the atomic unit of digital experiences, at the very core of what makes them work. Back-end engineers can help you develop a deep understanding of how you can use ways of linking data and objects to improve experiences. When I met the metadata engineer at my first full-time job, I sat down with her right away to find out all that our system knew to help me make decisions about navigation and page layout, and I've called on that knowledge again and again.

I WANT MY PRODUCT NOW!

Working with product managers can be one of the most difficult parts of UX. They are the keepers of the timeline and also have the primary responsibility for watching the budget, and both time and money concerns can be the enemies of good UX. Product managers are always on the lookout for scope creep, which is related to feature creep and often caused by it, but means the expansion of the original plan for a product that impacts multiple layers of work. From a UX perspective, if users love a feature introduced by some successful app, we want to see if there's any good way to work that feature into our developing product, especially if we learn a competitive product has done so or is about to come out with it. It can seem as if all the product manager sees, though, are the dollar signs and the ticking clock. With new devices and system updates constantly coming out, some product managers are concerned most of all with launching to more and more markets. And in my experience, UX concerns are the first to go by the wayside. I'll be frank; this can be infuriating.

But I also have to admit that pushback from product managers has made me better at what I do. Sometimes it's forced me to find a better, more cost- or time-effective way to do something. You must establish an agreed-upon set of user goals and business goals with your product manager early on, showing her your sketches or having a whiteboard session. As I've said before, the intersection of business and user goals is where UX can actually make the best contribution. The lesson I shared earlier—that goals specific only to the business should be strongly incentivized or otherwise integrated into the experience from the start, as opposed to being afterthoughts—was a hard one to learn, and it was a product manager who taught it to me.

It's best not to develop an adversarial relationship with your product managers, and finding ways to convey that you understand the constraints they are working with will help you gain their support. In making the case for my designs to product managers, I've found that two exercises can be very effective. The first was shown to me by a fellow General Assembly UX instructor and a member of the first YouTube design team, Hong Qu. It's a method of ranking all the features that might go into a product according to their anticipated usage, or actual usage if you're working on an update to a product. I refer to it as the Frequency versus Importance chart. You can see a sample chart in the next figure.

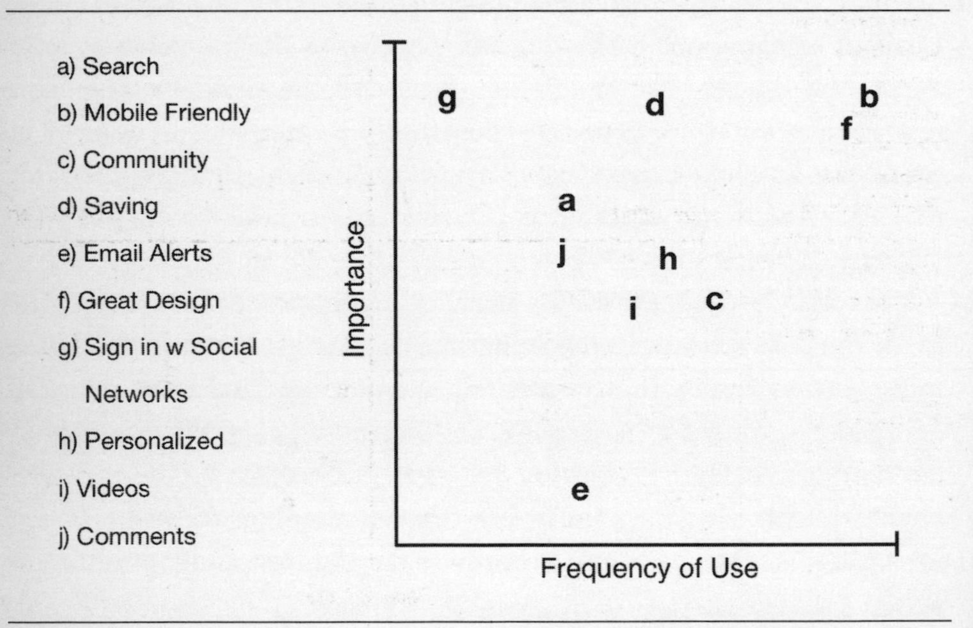

Frequency vs. Importance: *Give a set of features to users in friendly non-jargon terminology. Let them plot their answers in interviews and make their own. Use the individual responses during the interview as topics for investigation and in aggregate as trends in user input. Use discretion and abstract thinking to identify problems beyond the users' own concepts.*

Not only does creating this kind of chart help you refine your understanding of the users and their needs, but it can help to bring the whole team into alignment about priorities. It can be used as a baseline for discussing trade-offs among features and design improvements and can be very helpful in getting approval for the features you want from your product manager.

The other exercise I've found useful for making the case to product managers is an Effort versus Need chart, in which you compare an estimate of the effort needed to include a feature with how strong you believe the need for it is. The next figure shows an example.

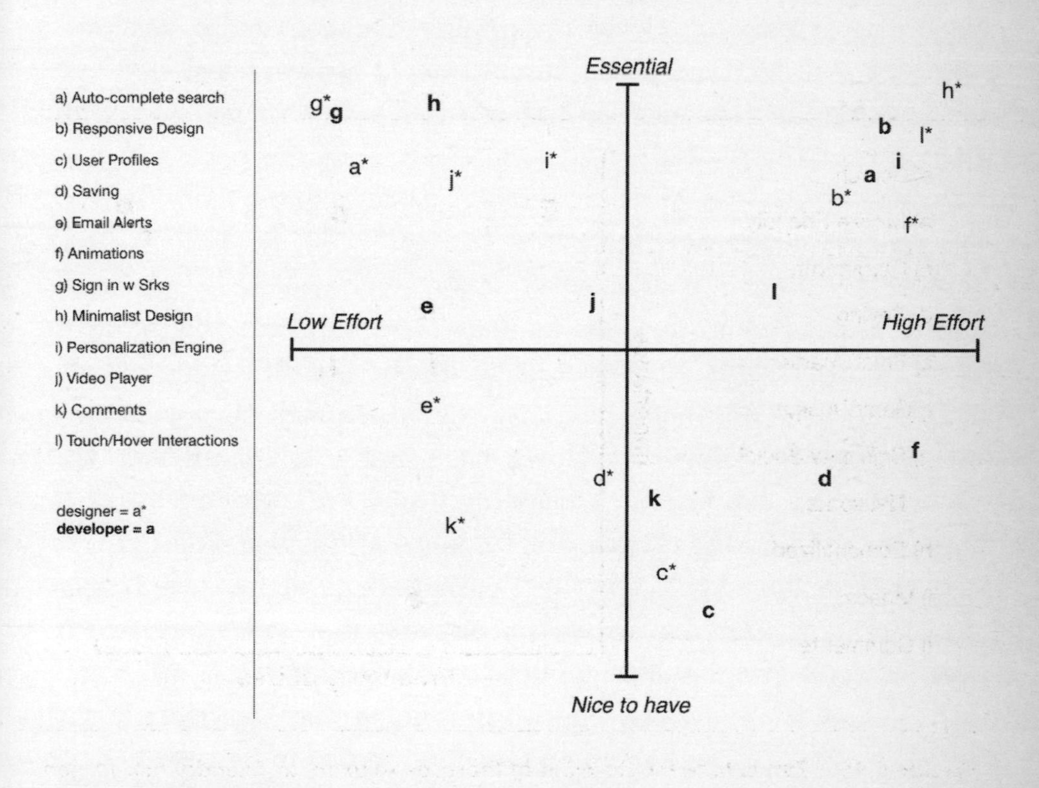

Effort vs. Need: *List out the features of a product in all their specificity and plot them on the graph according to your professional responsibilities. This chart shows a set plotted by both a designer and developer for a single set of features.*

Need is subjective, but good to clarify especially from a planned UX designer because high polish means multiple rounds of design and development. When plotted against each other the effort needed to create features gets priority from informed decisions and clarity of process objectives.

Creating this chart speaks powerfully about your respect for your team members' time and for the budget and time constraints to which your product manager is responsible for holding the project. You should get your estimates for the development time from your developers, but be aware that they will need to know enough about the design of the features to do a realistic job of estimating. Taking the time to make this chart has helped me to realize that I've got to streamline a design and drop or simplify features, and it has gone over very well with my product managers. I am confident that you will find that the time spent on both of these tools pays you back with interest.

COLLABORATION GOES BOTH WAYS

Always keep in mind that just as your team can help you, so does your UX expertise have quite a bit to offer them. The more collaborative you are with them, the more your team members will come to appreciate the value of UX over time. For visual designers, the UX perspective can help keep usability issues squarely in focus. UX input can also help them champion elements of the visual design that might be questioned by the product manager and higher-ups. If user tests show that users are responding strongly to a home page that is more minimal than the sales or marketing team might like, for example, and that it's effectively engaging users to move to parts of the site the business wants them to go to, that's going to be very helpful in getting the design approved. If the UX review of competitor sites reveals that your leading rival has seen a good uptick in users after a design update, that could be good support for making design changes the visual designer or team may have been pushing for.

I take the stance that my work with the designers who produce the visual assets for production is about providing evidence for their hypotheses. This has made designers more receptive to the user feedback I gather if a design tests poorly.

For front-end developers, with product managers always on alert for feature creep, UX data showing that users really like a given feature or are missing a feature they enjoy on other sites or apps can smooth the way toward approval. Data showing that a feature increases engagement or improves sales is the most potent. Maybe UX research shows that if animation is added to an interface, user clicks to deeper sections of the site go way up. Done!

As for product managers, a core part of their mandate is making sure that a product is appealing to users. This is why many product managers do some UX work themselves, such as conducting user interviews and creating personas. User interviews and personas didn't begin with the emergence of UX; they've been a staple of market research in product development for years. User testing is also run by product managers at many companies. In fact, at startups and smaller firms, the roles of PM and UX are often done by one person because they're so aligned. If there is a dedicated UX designer, though, and the UX work reveals that the A version of a design is twice as effective as the B version or that users are fleeing from a proposed redesign of a feature, any good product manager is going to appreciate the value of that information. And a UX designer can free up a good deal of time for the product manager so she can turn her attention to dealing with the other issues and groups she has to work with, such as marketing and the upper management.

EVERYONE CAN DO AT LEAST SOME UX

All of these reasons why it's valuable for UX designers to seek out collaboration with team members are also reasons why anyone in digital product development, no matter what role, should learn at least some of what UX is all about, even if they don't actually learn to apply the methods.

UX designers are not some exotic tribe from an island all their own; they are just people with some good UX training and experience. The fact that everyone on a team has some expertise they can bring to the UX process goes to show that it makes great sense for people to make their way into the work from a wide range of prior non-UX experience. It will not only help them to do their current jobs better but also their past experience will help them to do UX work better. I certainly wish I had known more about interfaces when I started. I had to put myself through that intensive self-taught method of obsessively redrawing dozens of interface designs to really understand them as a medium.

If you're a visual designer, incorporating UX methods into your work will enhance your ability to please and inspire users with your designs by tapping into their emotions and putting yourself in their place. It will also help you in presenting your design concepts and gaining support for them. If you're a front-end developer, UX practices are an especially natural add-on and you're definitely going to want to build up a good base of UX knowledge. Not only will it help you create more effective and pleasing interfaces, but it's becoming more expected by both firms and clients that UX will be part of what you'll bring to the process. The hybrid role of UX developer is rapidly gaining ground, and people with these combined skills are likely to be in increasingly high demand.

Back-end engineers can benefit from developing a deeper understanding of UX concerns by being better able to propose improvements to the design of products based on their systems knowledge. Learning to put themselves into the shoes of the wide range of users will help them anticipate ways in which the product should be able to provide users with information they'll want and to factor those issues in from the very start of the back-end planning.

For product managers, given the overlap with the missions and tools of UX design, learning more of the evaluation methods of UX makes great sense, and at plenty of companies, product managers are now expected to oversee UX work for projects. I think the part of UX that product managers would benefit most from is defining personas. Studying user flows, sketching page designs, and providing guidance on where design and system decisions fall in order of importance are also great enhancements of the product manager's core skill set. Wireframing and prototyping probably isn't necessary because there are generally going to be designers who can do those jobs, but knowing the ins and outs of how to read wireframes and what to ask for in a prototype are essential.

MAKING IT LEAN

Fitting the parts of UX that you think will be most beneficial into your skill set and working process is exactly what's being done with the increasingly popular practice of Lean UX. The method was created because development teams working on faster and faster production cycles have found it difficult to incorporate UX research and design time into the process. This has been especially true for teams switching to the Agile method of rapid-cycle, iterative development.

Born out of frustration with the older, sequential Waterfall approach (which moves slowly, step by step from requirements gathering, to design, to programming, and then testing and debugging), Agile breaks the work up into small units executed by cross-functional and self-managed teams, with designers and front- and back-end programmers all working together. The way the Agile method is practiced varies from company to company, but at its heart is the dividing up of design and development work into small increments called sprints, and the rapid coding and testing of those increments as work proceeds. This makes fitting UX research and design methods into the process difficult. Lean UX is a great solution, developed out of both the Agile method and the Lean Startup approach to product development.

The Lean Startup approach is also one of rapid development and testing in iterative cycles. Created by entrepreneur Eric Ries, author of the book *The Lean Startup*, the method combines the principles of rapid development cycles and testing from Agile with lessons from the Lean Manufacturing process developed at Toyota, which is focused on stripping out all wasted time and resources in manufacturing. Key foci of the Lean method are lowering the amount of inventory of parts that must be on hand for the assembly process and maintaining quality control throughout the process, catching any problems as early as possible.

The Lean Startup method focuses on the rapid creation of a minimum viable product (MVP), which might be thought of as a prototype, depending on which definition of prototype you mean. An MVP isn't meant to be a rough approximation of a product; it's meant to be a fully functioning product that can be distributed or offered to customers and from which a startup can gather real-world user feedback for testing the market and further developing the product. Ries calls this process "validated learning." You can see the relevance of UX. Core to the Lean Startup philosophy is that it's best to get actual user feedback about a product as early as you can.

So what exactly is Lean UX? The focus, according to UX designer Jeff Gothelf, who wrote the book *Lean UX*, is on doing away with many of the more time-consuming deliverables of UX design, like personas and wireframes, in order to get to the creation of a working prototype—or MVP—as fast as possible, to test that with customers, and then to iterate improvements. The process as Gothelf describes it involves quickly and roughly developing the concept for the product, generally by sketching, whether on paper or whiteboard, then moving right on to creating a prototype. After the prototype is internally approved, it is sent to the client or customers for testing and validated learning, and the product is then improved accordingly.

Some in the UX field would argue that this isn't "real" UX because it leaves so much out, but most UX work can, in fact, still be fit into this process, and the full, formal bag of UX skills will be valuable in making it work well. I think it's a good solution for companies that don't have the time or resources for a full-time UX researcher.

The rough conceptualization of the product should be a good sketch that also has some written explanation about the functionality to guide the creation of the prototype. The prototype should be robust enough to allow for valuable customer feedback—you don't want to provoke the kind of one-star reviews that litter app stores. The research usually done in UX design, including the creation of personas and competitive analysis, is still also valuable here and achievable in the Lean methodology; it just needs to be done without formalized presentations and reviews. Brief stories that specify a user's motivation and task is a good replacement. Interpreting customer feedback and devising the solutions for the next iteration are also right at the core of UX work. A special note is that because the process moves so much more quickly, collaboration among team members is especially important. As I've been stressing, this collaboration is in no way a violation of the UX process; quite the contrary. The more UX is understood not as the sum of its methodological parts, but as an effort to bring creativity, sensitivity to user needs, and systems expertise to bear on creating great products, the better for users and for those of us advocating for it.

SEEK INSPIRATION EVERYWHERE

Just as you should seek inspiration and insight from your team members, you should always be looking for ideas outside the office, out from behind the computer screen and in the world. You never know where good ideas are going to come from. There is so much emphasis in the writing about UX on getting to know users and their needs, and I just want to highlight that tapping into users' lives and experiences with your products should by no means define the limits of your idea horizons. You want to be drawing on all sorts of other sources of inspiration. As I said, UX design is not the sum of its methodologies; it's also a way of thinking and seeing. Once you start doing it, you'll find yourself almost constantly making note of useful and creative features you might work into your designs, from all over, including from totally outside the world of tech. Maybe that's an art exhibition you go to that uses videos in some way you might draw on, or a restaurant that has introduced some special element in its service that you can create a version of, say a friendly greeting to patrons printed on its menus or engaging explanations about the dishes offered.

One of my favorite ideas for a feature came from way outside of tech and had nothing to do with user interviews or personas. The app No Man's Land, created by my company, Tumbleweed, is an entertainment experience—some call it a game, but it started as an idea for a movie. I and my compadres in developing it never had any intention of turning it into an app. A few dozen of my friends and I thought it would be fun to collaborate on making a film, and each of us pitched in our personal time and money. I rented a small room in my apartment to be used as an editing room, and whoever had time could come work on the project. Different members of the team contributed to the editing, color correction, or whatever they could. As one of my future cofounders and I were talking one day, the idea popped into our heads to release the movie not as a standalone thing to visit and watch on the Internet but as something we could make way more interesting, more of an experience. We were on our way to lunch when the idea hit. What if it was a location-based movie? What if you had to be somewhere specific to watch each scene? Over the next several months we planned and researched and designed until we had what is now our very own location-based movie app.

Steve Jobs famously took inspiration from the calligraphy course he enrolled in at Reed College. As he told Stanford graduates in his famous commencement speech:

> I learned about serif and sans serif typefaces, about varying the amount of space between different letter combinations, about what makes great typography great. It was beautiful, historical, artistically subtle in a way that science can't capture.... When we were designing the first Macintosh computer, it all came back

to me. And we designed it all into the Mac. It was the first computer with beautiful typography.[2]

I love what he says about the poetry of type, but I disagree with him that science isn't capable of capturing such beauty and lyricism. When I think of naturally occurring geometric patterns or forces of nature that create perfect circles, such as the rings of Saturn, I can't help but think of the detailed observations needed to see forces behind these phenomena. I don't know if it's the kid in me or the scientist, but the artistry all around us in nature is just waiting to be explored.

The natural world and the science that has done so much to illuminate its workings are fantastic sources of inspiration for product

(Courtesy of NASA)

design. The field of biomimicry is all about that. An engineer in Japan used the shape of the kingfisher bird's beak as the model for a new design for the front of high-speed trains that allowed the trains to travel 10 percent faster while using 15 percent less electricity. Some software designers drew on lessons about how the internal structure of tree trunks is optimized for strength to design car bodies that are both more crash-proof and 30 percent lighter.[3] Conservationist and science writer Janine Benyus has a great TED talk about biomimicry titled "Biomimicry in Action" in which she discusses a number of other such examples.

Math, biology, astronomy, and even human sciences like sociology and psychology explore beautiful parts of our world, and all of them are great sources of inspiration for UX. The psychologist Robert Cialdini, author of the book *Influence: The Psychology of Persuasion*, has conducted fascinating research into the most effective ways to write messages with which we would like to stimulate some behavior, such as conserving electricity. In one experiment he found that if a sign on the bathroom counter in a hotel room said that the majority of the other guests who had stayed in that room had reused their bath towel at least once during their stay, significantly more guests would also reuse their towels during a stay, while a sign that asked guests to help the hotel conserve water by reusing their towels had significantly less effect. Imagine how valuable his findings are for writing good copy in software products.

I told the story of the Dallas airport redesign earlier. Well, airports are a fascinating source of ideas because they have to direct people where to go, and those people are often in a real hurry. Also, international airports in particular have to guide people who speak a wide range of languages and may not recognize the language of the country the airport is in. Anyone who has flown much knows that some airports do this much better than others. I was in the Dubai airport at the time of finishing this book and marveled at the big touch screen maps that show where gates are. Great UX. But they also have scanners for reading your boarding pass, to show you the right gate, and when I tried this, the scan failed—and no information was given about where to go to locate your gate if the scan didn't work. This was a great reminder that sometimes it takes only one flaw for a great UX idea to crash and burn.

The design of theme parks is a treasure trove of ideas for designing children's apps, as the Netflix example I gave earlier shows. The designers who came up with the idea of using beloved characters as guides may not have drawn the concept from Disney World, but the resulting experience is certainly an online version of the larger-than-life-sized Disney characters who greet entrants to the Magic Kingdom.

Being a New Yorker, I'm fascinated by the signs in subways in New York and around the world and how sign placement and clarity of message can make the difference between people taking the uptown train when they want to go downtown, as often happens in the New York system, or easily figuring out how to make their way through many twists and turns to switch from one line to another, as in the bowels of the London tube system.

Honing your ability to recognize great examples of user experience design all over your world and break them down into their essentials should be part of the daily routine of anyone who wants to be a good UX designer. And a vital part of this learning is to make astute translations into the software environment, not cumbersome ones.

I've referred many times in this book to video games as inspirations for UX, and of course gamification is becoming increasingly popular. It's also become a four-letter word to some, so I think a little discussion of how to do it well and where it goes off the rails fits into this discussion.

Foursquare is a company that has made an interesting go of it, and it is cited often in the discussion of the rise and fall of gamification. The app, by rewarding people for checking into locations with points and badges and allowing them to become the "mayor" of a place, built up a huge following of smartphone owners early, every advertiser's dream market. In fact, the app's success with the concept is part of the reason gamification has become so popular in UX design.

A former coteacher of mine at General Assembly, Alex Sarlin, begins his lecture on gamification in digital products by pointing out that games have developed such avid fans because they've tapped into the neurological channel that releases the pleasure-inducing neurotransmitter dopamine into our brains. They are the ultimate in goal- and reward-based behavior. Every time our avatars leap a tall building or shoot down a helicopter with a shoulder-fired missile, we get another dopamine hit, and this creates a powerful feedback loop. But the real artistry doesn't come from just offering rewards; it's in getting the blend of challenge and reward just right. The powerful pull of a task that requires full engagement because of the skill needed for execution was explored by the Hungarian psychologist Mihaly Csikszentmihalyi, who developed the theory of flow, the cognitive state we find ourselves in when we are engaged in such a task and are totally absorbed. Our perception of time is warped, and when we emerge from the state, hours may have passed when we think it's been only a short time. Video games have harnessed the power of flow brilliantly. The better you are at a game, the higher the level you move to, and you are back to that exquisite balance of challenge and reward that is optimal for flow.

Now consider Foursquare's version of gaming. Checking into more locations more often than your friends is hardly very challenging, not enough to keep the game alive. Over time, the badges and points just began to seem manipulative, and Foursquare deemphasized the game elements of the experience. This doesn't mean that all uses of elements of gaming have to induce a state of flow to be good UX, not at all. The point is that Foursquare failed to capture the true spirit of the goal-oriented incentivizing that makes games work. A much better way to use gamification is to help users learn about a site or app in a way that's both playful and more effective than the typical tutorials or labels and pop-ups.

SHOW, DON'T TELL

In the beginning, video games were all about telling a story. *Mario Bros.*, *Pac-Man*, and *Galaga* all told beginning, middle, and end stories. The beginning in each game integrated education and storytelling in a simple and direct way. If you didn't move, you died, and the story started over. This was an early manifestation of a dictum stressed in the interface guidelines of iOS7 and Android: "Let users interact with the content." Rather than making our products overtly teacherly in style, we should make them teach by interacting.

As game design has progressed, designers have expanded on the methods of educating users through creative use of UI. This means that in the mobile space especially, where touch interactions rule, there's still a great deal to be learned from games. One of my favorite examples is the way the video game *Dead Space* teaches users how to interact with the touch controls on the iPad. When you first load the game, after going through the menus and getting started, you are presented with a third-person view of your character standing in a room, from behind him. A moment later a green dot about the size of a dime starts moving around and creates a line of arrows that follow the dot's movement. You find you're drawn to interact with the dot, and when you put your finger on it and start moving it, your character begins to move around the room accordingly, and voilà, you have learned how to control your character in this new touch interaction environment. This kind of learning-by-doing interaction is one of the most effective ways to teach. Teaching by delighting, as *Dead Space* does, is even better, and should be a goal of every UX designer. And there is no manipulation involved here.

UX IS EVOLUTIONARY

The last thing I want to highlight is that UX will continue to evolve, and that just as computers are becoming ever more pervasive and are being woven into the fabric of our lives in continually more seamless ways, UX is likely to become more seamlessly woven into the skills of all those involved in product development, whether for web and app products, nontech products, or the fast-evolving set of products that combine both. Just consider the rapidly developing "Internet of Things." More and more of the devices in our lives are going to be hooked up to the Internet so that they can perform enhanced functions for us, such as TVs that remember what we've been watching, trash cans that warn us when the garbage needs to be taken out, cars that drive themselves, and buildings that automatically adjust window shades according to the progression of the sun during the day. Another recently introduced example is "smart" Christmas tree lights that perform a light show to the rhythm of whatever music you play. On a more serious note, GE has described a future digital "care traffic control system" for hospitals that will keep track of where all of the equipment needed for patient care is in the hospital and whether it's in use. Such a system will allow for much more effective allocation, so that when a patient needs a defibrillator right away, she's more likely to get it right away.

It's a great time to be interested in how computers and people interact. I'm a sucker for the future, and I'm excited by the potential of rapidly improving web technologies that can connect to the nonsilicon world. The better our computers get at sensing our environments and following us around, the more fun we'll get to have as UX designers.

I'm also a fan of people. I like meeting new people and talking to them in their natural habitats where they're comfortable. I like to observe people and learn about their worlds and habits and what makes them who they are. All that's really needed to get started in UX design is an enthusiasm for human behavior; all you need to know about the technology follows from there. The most essential qualification for becoming a good UX designer is the desire to help people improve their lives by making the computing technology that has become so pervasive serve their needs with intelligence, elegance, an edge of delight, and utter clarity. As John Maeda, a former president of the prestigious Rhode Island School of Design, wrote in his book *The Laws of Simplicity*, "The best art makes your head spin with questions. Perhaps this is the fundamental distinction between pure art and pure design. While great art makes you wonder, great design makes things clear."[4]

POINTS TO REMEMBER

Good UX Comes from Being Open to Input

- Be sure to tap the talents of everyone on your team; be open to input and don't think that you "own" the UX. The more that all team members understand the UX goals and contribute to them, the better.
- Collaboration can be challenging, so learning to speak the languages of all the players on the team and to appreciate their perspectives and challenges is important. The more you do so, the more receptive they will be to your UX ideas and the better they'll be able to help you realize them.
- Collaboration goes both ways, and you should always be looking for ways that your UX data and insights can help others on the team solve problems and make the case for their work.
- If the team you're in doesn't have the time and resources for a fuller UX process, consider using the Lean UX approach.
- Always keep your eyes and ears open for inspiration out and about in the world; it can come from the most unexpected places and in the briefest of moments. Constantly be looking for ideas from other domains that you can translate into your product.

NOTES

Chapter 1: Seeing Through Users' Eyes

1. David Hirsch, *The Deconstruction of Literature: Criticism After Auschwitz* (Hanover, NH: University Press of New England, 1991), 68.

2. Jim Carlton, "Befuddled PC Users Flood Help Lines, and No Question Seems to Be Too Basic," *Wall Street Journal*, March 1, 1994, page B1.

3. RinkWorks.com, "Computer Stupidities: Icons," http://www.rinkworks.com/stupid/cs_icons.shtml.

4. Clifford Nass with Corina Yen, *The Man Who Lied to His Laptop* (New York: Penguin Group USA), 2.

5. Scott Simon, "It's a Girl! The New iPhone Speaks," *Simon Says* (blog), October 22, 2011, www.npr.org/2011/10/22/141613679/its-a-girl-the-new-iphone-speaks.

6. Dirk Heylen, Betsy van Dijk, and Anton Nijholt, "Robotic Rabbit Companions: Amusing or a Nuisance?" *Journal of Multimodal User Interfaces* 5 (2012), 53–59, doi: 10.1007/s12193-011-0083-3, http://link.springer.com/content/pdf/10.1007%2Fs12193-011-0083-3.pdf.

7. Jakob Nielsen and Don Norman, "The Definition of User Experience," Nielsen Norman Group, www.nngroup.com/articles/definition-user-experience/.

8. Jakob Nielsen, "Usability 101: Introduction to Usability," Nielsen Norman Group, January 4, 2012, http://www.nngroup.com/articles/usability-101-introduction-to-usability/.

Chapter 2: Creativity Loves Constraints

1. Android Design, "Design Principles," http://developer.android.com/design/get-started/principles.html.

Chapter 3: Interface Designs Are the Facial Expressions of Digital Products

1. Rachel Hinman, "A New Mobile UX Design Material," Smashingmagazine.com, October 30, 2012, http://www.smashingmagazine.com/2012/10/30/motion-and-animation-a-new-mobile-ux-design-material/.

2. Bill Buxton, *Sketching the User Experience* (Burlington, MA: Morgan Kaufmann Publishers, 2007), 153.

3. Antoine de Saint-Exupéry, *Wind, Sand and Stars* (Boston: Harcourt Brace Jovanovich, 1992), 42.

Chapter 4: Innovation Is Not for Innovation's Sake

1. Dylan Love and Gus Lubin, "13 First-to-Market Products That Failed," *Business Insider*, May 25, 2011, http://www.businessinsider.com/first-to-market-products-that-failed-2011-5?op=1.

2. Facebook, "Investor Relations," http://investor.fb.com/results.cfm.

3. Adam Lashinsky, "Amazon's Jeff Bezos: The Ultimate Disrupter," CNN Money, November 16, 2012, http://management.fortune.cnn.com/2012/11/16/jeff-bezos-amazon/.

4. Kurt Wagner, "Facebook Launches Redesigned Mobile App for iOS 7," *Mashable*, September 18, 2013, http://mashable.com/2013/09/18/facebook-app-ios-7/.

Chapter 5: Good UX Comes from Being Open to Input

1. John Donne, "Meditation XVII," *Devotions Upon Emergent Occasions* (New York: Random House, 1999), 1103.

2. Steve Jobs, Commencement Address, Stanford University, June 12, 2005, text available at http://news.stanford.edu/news/2005/june15/jobs-061505.html.

3. Biomimicry Institute, "CAO and SKO Design Software," http://www.asknature.org/product/99d6740a0a07a9d003480f1c414ee177.

4. John Maeda, *The Laws of Simplicity* (Boston: MIT Press, 2006), 70.

INDEX

Page numbers of illustrations appear in *italics*.

ABOUT THE AUTHOR

Luke Miller is a user experience designer and researcher. He began his career in UX with the *Wall Street Journal*, and in the beginning of 2013 he moved on to help form the new Yahoo! mobile product office in New York. In the same year he cofounded Tumbleweed, a production studio that makes mobile storytelling experiences.

In addition to teaching UX design classes at General Assembly, Luke also teaches a mobile-specific course at Parsons, the New School for Design. He is a guest lecturer at Columbia Business School and mentors startups, entrepreneurs, and design professionals. He holds an MS in information science from the University of North Carolina in Chapel Hill. You can tweet him @younglucas and find him at General Assembly in New York most weekends.